SECRETS OF THE INNER SELF

The Complete Book of Numerology

Dr David A. Phillips

ANGUS & ROBERTSON PUBLISHERS

ANGUS & ROBERTSON PUBLISHERS
London • Sydney • Melbourne

First published by Angus & Robertson Publishers, Australia, 1980
This paperback edition 1981
Reprinted 1981, 1983

© David A. Phillips 1980

National Library of Australia
Cataloguing-in-publication data.
Phillips, David
  Secrets of the inner self.
  ISBN 0 207 14760 4
  1. Symbolism of numbers.
  I. Title
133.3′35

Printed by The Dominion Press - Hedges & Bell
Maryborough, 3465

CONTENTS

INTRODUCTION

Be prepared. You are about to embark on the most exciting of all journeys — the discovery of who you are. Many people pass through life making only little progress in this vital investigation. Others appear to achieve a certain success in worldly terms, in spite of being comparatively ignorant of who they really are, where they are going, and how they should handle the problems along the Path.

Can you imagine how much greater success would be achieved if, in their climb up the ladder of success, people had a reliable form of guidance? This guidance is readily and easily available to all who seek it. And you who are studying this book have qualified. As you explore these pages, investigating the science of numbers, you will see how easily and simply this system works. You will marvel at the guidance it brings in all aspects of life. You will want to check this system on yourself, on your family, and on your friends. You should do that at every opportunity for this practice will develop your confidence in the use of numerology and your understanding of the various aspects of human individuality so revealed.

To assist you in the practical application of these techniques, the birthdates of twenty-five famous people have been chosen to exemplify some of the numerological aspects revealed on the following pages. Each person is considered to be famous for certain successes they have achieved in life.

Ludwig Van Beethoven Born December 16, 1770. Beethoven's genius as a musical composer is undisputed, yet his personal life was little short of a tragedy. We shall investigate the reasons and learn the factors which earned him a place in the heart of every music lover.

Joh Bjelke-Petersen Born January 13, 1911. One of this country's most controversial state premiers, the present premier of Queensland is by far the most outspoken politician in Australia today. Most people have no doubt of their feelings regarding this man: they either respect and admire him or they loathe and detest him. What makes a person so forthright?

Napoleon Bonaparte Born August 15, 1769. The subject of the dedication of Beethoven's famous Eroica Symphony until he declared himself emperor of France and lost favour with the composer, Napoleon was regarded as the most skilled military leader of the century. He was also the most misunderstood and feared of rulers. Was he a hero or a villain?

Richard Bonynge Born September 29, 1930. Famous English musician and orchestral conductor, whose marriage to Joan Sutherland brought to them both a degree of fame rarely equalled in the musical world.

Ita Buttrose Born January 17, 1942. As publisher of The Australian Women's Weekly, Ita Buttrose is considered one of the most influential and most powerful women of the Australian media. She is certainly one of the most interesting and self-motivated women in Australian public life.

Forbes Carlisle Born June 3, 1921. One of Australia's leading all-round sportsmen, Forbes Carlisle's more recent fame has come from his training of Australia's leading young swimmers. Through his unique ability to develop and employ innovative methods he has been responsible for creating more swimming stars than any other coach.

Winston Churchill Born November 30, 1874. Statesman, orator, writer and painter, the most famous British prime minister this century gave the world a model of courageous stamina and dynamic assertiveness. Many would say that he singlehandedly led Britain through the dark hours of World War II, to its decisive conclusion in 1945. Perhaps one of his saddest moments was when his party suffered post-war defeat at the general election and he resigned as prime minister. It was not so much the result of the disapproval of an unappreciative public as the typical sacrifice to be found in the life of a Ruling 7 who has much learning to do.

Don Dunstan Born September 21, 1926. Even as one of the most influential politicians in Australia in the 1970s, Don Dunstan's talents were not to be limited — he is also an accomplished actor and poet. It is fascinating to see how these diverse talents are revealed in his numerological analysis and how his surprise resignation as premier of South Australia will affect the expression of these talents.

Malcolm Fraser Born May 21, 1930. Commanding the highest political position in Australia since 1975, Malcolm Fraser's rise to political prominence was both speedy and dramatic. He is regarded by many as an enigma, which is not surprising when we recognise some of his deeper personality aspects, as revealed in his numerological analysis.

Indira Gandhi Born November 19, 1917. Undoubtedly the most controversial female head of government of modern times, Mrs Gandhi is known to possess a deep understanding of her country's needs, but has been unwise in her methods. Her numerological analysis throws light upon her personality problems and what has driven her to become the most dynamic personality in the world's largest democracy.

Germaine Greer Born January 29, 1939. Certainly one of the most outspoken feminists of all time, Ms Greer has proven the effective role women can play in determining the direction of human thought by her brilliant literary efforts. Analysing her birthdate reveals the driving force within this unique Australian.

Lang Hancock Born June 10, 1909. His discovery of vast mineral wealth in Western Australia has made Lang Hancock one of Australia's richest men — and one of the most listened to. His outspoken concern for the direction of this country's future and his intense involvement in its development are indicative of a person who has discovered his Path. Such a discovery is available to every student of the science of numbers.

Bob Hawke Born December 9, 1929. The most famous and self-motivated champion of the Australian worker, Bob Hawke is also a brilliant academic, debater, and negotiator. But he has some serious problems to overcome as he prepares to enter a new phase of his life in federal politics. Will he allow us to help him?

Xavier Herbert Born May 15, 1901. He is one of Australia's leading authors and has undertaken a considerable amount of work to assist the Aborigines rediscover their identity and self-respect. His is a life of sheer determination, as revealed so clearly in his numbers.

Caroline Jones Born January 1, 1938. This lady has established a reputation as one of Australia's leading broadcasters and media interviewers. Her programmes on A.B.C. radio and television command nation-wide audiences and her attitude to life reflects a unique level of balance and happiness.

Edward Kennedy Born February 22, 1932. Leading American senator, born on the birthday of George Washington, Teddy Kennedy is also one of his country's most controversial public figures. He is one of the wealthiest men in America and also, perhaps, one of the most confused. However, his decision to enter the 1980 presidential race indicates that he has entered a more decisive period, although it certainly will not be any happier for him.

Wolfgang Amadeus Mozart Born January 27, 1756. Recognised as one of the most influential composers of all time, Mozart's musical career commenced at age three. At five he had written his first composition and by twenty-one had composed more than 200 musical works. He was one of the finest pianists, organists and violinists of his day. In his thirty-five years his output of musical compositions exceeded 800 — a true musical genius.

Rupert Murdoch Born March 11, 1931. Without a doubt he is Australia's best known media mogul, achieving worldwide repute for his imaginative and aggressive marketing and purchasing techniques. His newspaper chain extends throughout the United States and into Europe, making him one of the most influential men in the media world.

Sir Mark Oliphant Born October 8, 1901. A leading Australian scientist, Sir Mark has the unique distinction of having served as a state governor. His governorship of South Australia was marked by the same introspection, good judgement and care as his renowned scientific career.

Kerry Packer Born December 17, 1937. Another Australian influential in the media world, Kerry Packer inherited a vast newspaper, television and radio empire which, under his guidance, has expanded significantly. More recently, he has astonished the Anglo-Saxon world with his entry into the promotion of major sporting events.

Prince Philip Born June 10, 1921. As the husband of Queen Elizabeth II, Prince Philip would be expected to play a somewhat secondary role. Yet he achieves this with distinction, for his special personality traits have prepared him for a major supportive role. Although he is often in the world spotlight he usually manages to avoid controversy. Numerological analysis proves how eminently suitable he is for his demanding yet constrictive vocation.

Bertrand Russell Born May 18, 1872. One of the leading philosophers, historians and thinkers of his day, Lord Russell left a literary and academic legacy which extended even into political activism. All this was achieved despite a unique deficiency in his personal characteristics.

Joan Sutherland Born November 7, 1926. Undisputed prima donna in opera in the 1970s, Joan Sutherland is one of the greatest musical artists Australia has produced. Though endowed with one of the most remarkable voices of all time, she has achieved a level of supremacy which she could never have accomplished on her own.

<u>Margaret Thatcher</u>   Born October 13, 1925. The first female prime minister of Great Britain, Margaret Thatcher is a dynamic person with a reputation for determination, thoughtfulness and self-control. These are natural attributes to her, as we shall see from the analysis of her powerful birthdate.

<u>Michael Willesee</u>   Born June 29, 1942. Son of a prominent Labor politician, Michael has achieved an even greater nationwide recognition in his role as a leading broadcaster and interviewer. His mental alertness and acute sense of fair play have been his constant guides in exposing many frauds.

STAGE 1
How it Came to Be

Man know thyself; then thou shalt know the Universe and God.'
                                    Pythagoras, 598-504 B.C.

Within each person is a beautiful light just waiting to shine forth, a beautiful being just aching for expression. Each person is really two people — that which we freely express is the image; that which we suppress all too frequently is the real person, the Inner Self. In associating with other people and through exposure to our environment, we become known by the image we create. This is not the real self. Rather, is it an emotional ghost we have cultivated to defend our sensitivities. But we sell ourselves far too short, for the image can never hold a light to the beauty and grandeur of the Inner Self. It is time for the Inner Self to become less of a stranger. Its acute sensitivity is so often mistaken for vulnerability, causing it to be encircled by our psychological wall. In that manner, it is stifled. It needs airing, exercise, expression. We commence to discover the secrets of the Inner Self when we start to understand who we are, from whence we have come, our purpose and where we are going. Answers to these investigations remain secrets only so long as we fail to discover the deep, yet profoundly simple meaning of life.

In different ways, we are all searching. Some people search unconsciously, being hardly aware of the search and less aware of what they seek. Others are searching blindly, looking for something which they would fail to recognise even if found, for they keep hoping it is a pot of gold at the end of the rainbow. Religions and politicians keep these hopes alive, always promising something better but never seeming to deliver the goods. Thinking, sensitive people need more answers to life; they need guidance, not promises. It is this common need which has brought us together to this point.

In the early 1950s, while still an undergraduate, my own searching led me from the maze of physical sciences to a point where mathematics and philosophy met. Here, I rediscovered Pythagoras. It was as though the missing pieces had been

1

uncovered. Life's jigsaw puzzle at last became a picture of beauty. Numbers commenced to come to life. They cast off the limitations of mere measurement to which modern science had unthinkingly relegated them, resuming their role as symbols, custodians of the keys to higher knowledge. Numbers became recognised as the hieroglyphs of infinite knowledge, representing the many human and environmental characteristics we soon propose to analyse and understand. Our method of achieving this is through an understanding of the symbols by which these qualities appear in life. Pythagoras recognised these symbols in numbers. Employing simple numbers, he formulated a system by which 'the unknown became known'. Pythagoras called this system 'mathematics'.

Modern mathematics throw no light on the solving of life's mysteries, nor do they attempt to unravel the secrets of the Inner Self. They are merely quantitative. They have evolved into a somewhat complex system for accounting, measuring and comparing, enabling you to count your money, calculate your tax, measure your land and compare today's temperature with the average; but they do not help you to overcome your sensitivity, guide you into your most suitable career, reveal the degree of compatibility between you and any other person, or recognise the most suitable time to change your job or to travel or get married. But the Science of Numbers, or qualitative mathematics, can do this. The Greeks, in their study of numbers, followed the tradition of the Phoenician sages and the Egyptian priests. They were the first race in historical times to recognise and employ the science of numbers as a means of discovering man's true identity, of revealing the secrets of his Inner Self in a manner which any thinking person could follow.

Born into a turbulent era of political despotism, Pythagoras as a youth recognised the need for man to gain precious freedom from slavery. This was itself a unique realisation for one born into a wealthy, highly intelligent family. But he recognised his calling and in 581 B.C., when a mere sixteen years of age, Pythagoras sailed from his native island of Samos to further his studies in Phoenicia, Egypt and Babylon. He returned to Samos in 545 B.C. to found his first university and simultaneously founded a new cultural era. But political disruptions forced the closure of the university after only two years.

It was not until 529 B.C. that Pythagoras finally persuaded a government to allow his philosophic system to prevail throughout its state. This was in the Greek colony of Crotona, located (even to this day) in southern Italy. For over twenty years this second, and most important, Pythagorean university flourished as the most progressive cultural centre then known. By admitting women as students equal to men, by excluding any discrimination based on

2

race, colour, political persuasion, religion or financial substance, this centre of learning became extremely popular, creating an entirely new standard which was to set the pattern for our twentieth century. By offering a curriculum of graduated teaching of all subjects influencing human life and welfare, ranging from the microcosmic to the macrocosmic, this university developed awareness of the sciences, arts and philosophy in a manner never previously encountered. At last, average people with a desire to learn could do so. This was indeed a universal concept both in its teaching and its membership. Pythagoras accepted into his university anyone prepared to undertake his discipline of learning. Students would invariably be surprised to find this encompassed investigations into the entire universe, both beyond and within man. Special emphasis was given to preparing the students for this 'new' form of learning by introducing them to a new set of guidelines by which their mental, emotional and physical attunements were developed. (Greater detail of these guidelines is contained in the author's book, From Soil to Psyche, Woodbridge Press, California, 1977.) This tradition (as it was destined to become) introduced many hitherto unrecognised aspects of human expression and personality. And when the same practice is employed today, humans discover so many secrets of their Inner Selves that life no longer remains a mystery.

Hence, by his unique studies, researches and tutoring, Pythagoras became known simultaneously as the founder of the scientific system, of modern mathematics, musical theory, philosophy and hygiene (the science of health). But his special achievement, in which our immediate interest lies, is his adaptation of the simple numerical system to a symbolic representation of human life and expression. It is essentially this same system we employ today in our mathematics and, numerologically, in our logical search for the meaning of life. Such revelation is the purpose of this book.

3

STAGE 2
The Basis of Personality

Man has made little progress in 2,500 years. We cannot deny life is physically easier, even though some people in authority would have us believe it was not meant to be that way. Firsthand contact with other heavenly bodies, instantaneous worldwide transmission of pictures and sounds, powerful machines for personal transport, etc., are but superficial developments of science. The really valuable application of science is to be attained, not by such superficialities, but in improving the quality of human life so that it may fulfil its purpose. Only in this manner can we achieve real happiness in life.

To seek a high level of financial security and a place in <u>Who's Who</u> are goals to which many people aspire. Others might seek a quiet little shack in the country with a few little pet animals and a few hectares of cultivated independence. All these are really extraneous. What we all seek is freedom from want, perfect health and appreciation for what we are and what we do. It is these alone which bring happiness to our Inner Selves. And it is this seeking which determines the manner in which we express ourselves. How we speak and act, therefore, creates the image by which we become known. Our expressions create the picture of ourselves that we present to the world. People accept this as our personality. But is it consistently the same in all situations?

As living becomes more complex with the increasing emphasis we place on time and money, our lives tend to 'departmentalise'. Different types of people associate with us in different walks of life, variations exist between those with whom we work, socialise, or meet in sports activities or studies. To each of these types of people we present a general image, yet change of environment often produces variations upon our general personality theme. Some people might see us as diligent, rather quiet and co-operative (if, for instance, we are working under direction in our employment); others might see us as aggressive, noisy and hyperactive (in our sporting activities, for example, if we excel at our game). At home, we might be submissive and even somewhat introverted (if, let's say, our spouse is domineering and the more eager to direct). Yet all

4

these variations are rooted in the same personality. So where is there a reliable basis upon which we can understand that personality?

In spite of the apparent complexities in the personality of the average person there is a sound basis for our analysis and understanding. The variations of actions and reactions from the one person are invariably consistent within the nature of his individuality. But then, the influences of environment and heredity play vital roles in helping to formulate the personality. Each of these factors needs investigation and analysis, of course, if we are to discover the essence of the personality. Each is a vital component in the representation of this personality, yet each exerts varying degrees of influence.

So that we may have a definite understanding of these various factors, the following diagram is offered as a general guide:

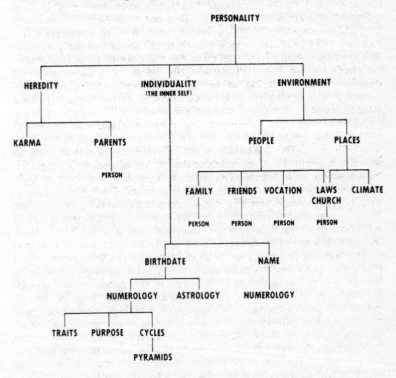

The diagram illustrates the three basic components and their varying influences on the development of the personality. Heredity and environment are largely external to the individuality, which is the essence of the Inner Self. The development of our individuality can be easily recognised and guided by a thorough understanding of our personal numerology. But the degree by which we allow this development to proceed is significantly influenced by the balance in our lives between action and reaction. To engage in action is to express and develop the individuality. It is directed from the Inner Self. The alternative is reaction — our responses to environmental and heredity factors, such as the influences of society, climate, family, karma, etc. It is vitally important to understand this distinction, for once we understand it, we recognise whether we are being true to ourselves or whether we are reflecting someone else or some past experience. Far too many people allow their individualities to be submerged within a mire of conformity.

How many of us are dissatisfied with the orthodox approach to life and dare to be different? Doubtless everyone reading this question will answer 'Well, I do'. This common need has actually brought us together to this point. So now we can commence the journey of self-discovery as we each learn about our individuality. We are not seeking to be different for the sake of difference itself, but because we have recognised the need for greater personal development. This being so, let us briefly look into the aspects of heredity and environment to ascertain the extent to which they influence our personalities and the extent to which they can limit us.

The karmic aspect of heredity implies a situation we created in former lives, generally in the last life, which we have brought forth into this one. The parental aspect of heredity is not limited to genetic functions. It exerts considerable influence during our development as a foetus, as a consequence of the prevailing mental, emotional and physical states of both parents. During our infancy, this 'environmental heredity' maintains a high level of strength; but this will gradually diminish as we become more exposed to environmental factors beyond parental limitations. The young individuality seeks to express itself but finds such strong external forces prevailing that for many years it must wait. Wise parents will recognise the need to train their newly incarnated responsibility from the very beginning of its life. For all too soon, environmental factors will exert their own pressures and may swamp the ill-prepared young psyche. Disciplined training, therefore, will strengthen the individuality and avoid the development of a reactive personality. It is impossible to express our individuality while simultaneously reflecting the mannerisms of other people, or reacting to the influence of environment. Rarely does growth take place in the shade (unless one happens to be a mushroom).

For individuality to develop, for the beauty of a vibrant personality to be expressed, we must free ourselves from any

6

limitations placed upon us by parents, friends and places. We must desist from seeking excuses, from justifying our habits and from the laziness of mimicry. We must look within ourselves to find the essence of our special individuality, to divest ourselves of the shackles of limitation and to discover that power of awareness which is really our intelligence in action.

As we proceed to attain an understanding of the Inner Self we spontaneously cast off any conditionings of environment and heredity which have previously limited us. Yet, there will be many influences which have proven quite valuable and others about which we might be a little unsure. Any uncertainty can be readily dispelled by applying the same numerological principles to them as we do to attaining the understanding of ourselves. Virtually all our environmental and heredity factors are people (the family, the boss, the spouse, etc.), and a system for analysing people is what we are now proposing to develop. When we learn to recognise what makes people tick, what constitutes the basis of each personality influencing us, we are in an ideal position to assess to what degree we shall allow such influence to have effect on our lives. We then act, rather than react. This is the expression of true individuality.

These are the secrets the science of numbers will now reveal to us. And wise use of this knowledge is an important responsibility we must each be prepared to accept.

STAGE 3
The Most Important Day

All energy is vibration. Everything, whether animate or apparently inanimate, is in a state of vibration. Every atom and the components of every atom are in a state of flux. Vibrations vary from one another by the frequency of their movement — expressed simply, by the number of cycles per second and by the size (amplitude) of that number. Variations between vibrations create individual aspects of life. If we could attain some concept of all the vibrations in creation we would better appreciate the limitlessness of the Creator. Every human being is different, the entire four thousand million of us. These differences give rise to human individuality. Our individuality varies in accordance with our personal vibrations and their power. Therefore, we must develop a means whereby these vibrations can be understood if we are to attain the key to human individuality and its relationship to environmental and heredity factors.

Is there any doubt that certain influences of heredity are exerted upon each of us before we are born? Karmic aspects of these influences have prevailed, with varying degrees of influence, from pre-prenatal times. However, as the soul continues to evolve to higher levels of awareness, through repeated incarnations, most major karmic debts are expiated during the lifetime in which they were created, leaving very little carry-over. For most people the more contemporary heredity, that engendered by their mother's emotional state while they were in the womb, will exert greater influence than will karma. Yet, as we have previously noted, even this influence will invariably diminish as infants develop into childhood with the growth of their own individuality.

There is a prevailing tendency amongst most academic and health authorities to confuse habit and heredity. This is a long-standing habit which has been brought into question over recent years. Blame not heredity, where so often habit is at fault.

> A fifteen-year-old arthritic patient was brought to me
> because her mother realised drugs could not permanently
> cure her problem. Melissa had been told by her general

practitioner that her condition was inherited (her parents were also arthritic, but not so severely). The child was following the same diet as her parents, although she did not enjoy eating meat. Analysing her birthdate, I quickly discovered Melissa's difficulty of self-expression, her deeply compassionate nature and exceptional sensitivity, which had developed into something of an inferiority complex. She ate her mother's cooking rather than try to prevail against dominant parents (as their numerological analyses revealed). Melissa's analysis also revealed her tendency towards hyperacidity, a precursor of arthritis.

The mother's birthdate told me of her overbalanced idealism and that she was motivated not so much by reason as by habit. Analysing the father revealed his intensely logical and critical approach to all things and his deep, though largely unexpressed, love for the home.

They were very quick to respond as patients, although a little slow to accept that arthritis is not an inherited problem but a function of diet and emotions.

It required only three consultations to steer the members of this family closer to their correct Paths. What commenced as a health matter concluded as a total reassessment of lifestyles. The parents became aware of Melissa's inner nature, the mother recognised her constant domination, the father his critical attitude, and the three, the need to increase fresh foods and reduce starches and meat in their diet.

Within a year their arthritic problems had vanished. They were also a far happier family group.

Modern studies clearly reveal how much mimicry infants employ. They learn far more from imitating parents' habits than has previously been recognised. With the parents representing the infants' first anchor of trust, it is little wonder that the children's subconscious attitude of 'if it is good enough for my parents, it is good enough for me' is so strong. (Hopefully with this realisation parents will assume a far greater responsibility for their words and actions). This attitude persists well past infancy. Some people maintain traces of it even into old age. But, fortunately, the development of the individuality contributes to a corresponding decrease in the influence of both actual (prenatal) and assumed (habit-oriented) heredity factors.

Individuality begins to stir at the birth of the infant. This is when its first independent movement is made, its first breath of fresh air is inhaled. As the umbilical cord is severed the infant commences to prepare itself for its first independent meal. It can now stretch without confinement in this bright new environment and can make all manner of sounds that are clearly audible. After all these months of darkness and confinement, it has commenced its individuality at last. Thus, the most important day in the entire life of a human being is the day upon which its individuality commences to develop — the day on which its individual life makes its debut. This is the day of birth. From that first day the new person makes his or her presence felt in the world. So begins the development of the personality. It is vitally important to recognise that personality is composed of individuality, tempered by environment and heredity. But the root material from which the personality unfolds is, unquestionably, the individuality.

The personality effectively becomes the expression of this individuality, an expression which develops its own special uniqueness as the child grows and becomes a part of its home environment and then of society. Therefore, to find the key to this personality, in order to discover the secrets of the Inner Self, we must understand the essence of the individuality. The science of numbers offers a very accurate means of analysing the individuality. This numerological method is not new, for we have seen how it developed at the very beginning of Western culture in the sixth century B.C.

Even predating this ancient science was that of astrology. Its origin is untraceable, but we know it can still give us many valuable insights into human life. Essentially physical scientists, together with some reporters, business people, etc., cogently deny any valid substance to astrology. But they should realise that it is unwise to condemn those things of which they have made no impartial study. Experience proves a very definite role for astrology in learning the secrets of the Inner Self. As will be seen further on, we employ the essential characteristics of the Sun Signs (Stage 11) to throw additional light upon our numerological analysis. These, too, are derived from the day of birth, the most important day in any life.

STAGE 4
The Ruling Numbers—Your Pathway in Life

'Evolution is the law of Life.
Number is the law of the Universe.
Unity is the law of God.'

> Pythagoras,
> as quoted by Edouard Schure,
> in his book, The Great Initiates.

We are all travellers on the Path. Some of us have stopped and are resting — indeed, too many have rested for too long. Some are making discursive detours into diverse tracks leading away from the Path, tracks which appear to offer many a rich inducement, yet resolve into nothing more than a confirmation that we have only one Path. (How long will these exercises in futility persist?) A patient recommended to me by her general practitioner was typical of the many who indulge in, or are forced to undertake, departures from their pristine Path.

Joyce had been under the care of her doctor for almost a year. Her lack of energy and repeated headaches superficially indicated hypoglycemia — low blood sugar. All sorts of pills, potions and placebos had been tried, so her referring doctor told me. He had also implemented some minor dietary changes for her, but Joyce was already on a healthy, natural foods diet.

Within seconds of numerologically setting up Joyce's birthdate, I asked if she felt she was being suppressed. Tears came into her eyes. Intuitively I asked for her husband's birthdate. Upon preparing his Birthchart, the answer was clear.

Here was a highly sensitive, thirty-nine-year-old woman who longed to be with people, to teach, to express herself in helping others, now that her children had grown up. But she had married an intensely possessive man of the old school. He wanted to remain the unquestioned family head and sole

11

breadwinner — thus keeping his wife dependent. Yet it also kept her from her Path.

This was a critical year for Joyce. She was on an important Peak of her Pyramids (as explained in Stage 10). A year of decision, indeed. She wisely decided to undertake a remedial teacher training course, to the accompaniment of fortissimo notes of marital discord. But Joyce found her strength of will and won through.

Now, two years later, she and hubby are happier than ever. She has an exciting job with handicapped children and is completely free of headaches, all the while enjoying so much energy that she feels twenty years younger.

Fortunately, there are some of us who are moving ever forward, who have discovered the Path and who will never leave it again. They know that to choose any alternative is to accept a lesser prospect. As we seek to recover unity with the Creator, we shed, one by one, all those cloaks of imagery with which we have dressed our appearance to the world. As they fall away, the growth of our real personality emerges, revealing the beautiful psyche, the core of our personal universe, our reason for being, as the French say, our raison d'etre. This personal evolution is our progress along the Path. And our Path is, as a matter of course, in total harmony with the law of the universe. It is, indeed, an integral part of that law which is best understood by medium of numbers, those symbols of its very essence.

Of fundamental importance is the number which will reveal to us the basic guidance for our life, the number of our Pathway. This we call our Ruling Number. It is that important number which is found by obtaining the total of each individual number in our birthdate and, in all instances but three, resolving it to a single digit number. The method is illustrated by the following examples:

If we take the birthdate of January 3, 1960 and rewrite it numerically as 1-3-1960, we find the total of the individual numbers when added comes to 20. This is done by adding the month number, 1, the day number, 3, and each of the numbers forming the year, giving us the simple arithmetical sum of:

$$1 + 3 + 1 + 9 + 6 + 0 = 20$$

This total of 20 is one of those that follows the rule of reduction to its single digit number, by adding each of its component numbers. Thus:

$$2 + 0 = 2$$

The inclusion of the zero does not alter the total, but it is shown in the two sums to avoid the usual question of what to do with the zero.

The Ruling Number of a person with the birthdate of January 3, 1960 is 2. In practice it is most convenient to write the birthdates and Ruling Number by placing the month first, then the day, followed by the year, in the following manner:

1-3-1960 = 20/2

Here is a series of birthdates to illustrate how each Ruling Number is arrived at:

February 2, 1960 — 2-2-1960 = 20/2   — Ruling Number of 2
February 3, 1960 — 2-3-1960 = 21/3   — Ruling Number of 3
February 3, 1979 — 2-3-1979 = 31/4   — Ruling Number of 4
February 4, 1970 — 2-4-1970 = 23/5   — Ruling Number of 5
February 5, 1970 — 2-5-1970 = 24/6   — Ruling Number of 6
February 7, 1969 — 2-7-1969 = 34/7   — Ruling Number of 7
February 8, 1969 — 2-8-1969 = 35/8   — Ruling Number of 8
February 9, 1969 — 2-9-1969 = 36/9   — Ruling Number of 9
February 1, 1969 — 2-1-1969 = 28/10   — Ruling Number of 10
February 2, 1969 — 2-2-1969 = 29/11   — Ruling Number of 11
February 2, 1962 — 2-2-1962 = 22/4   — Ruling Number of 22/4

Note that the Ruling Numbers used in this proven system of analysis commence with the number 2 and continue through each consecutive number to 11, then jump to 22/4, spoken of as twenty-two four. No Ruling Number 1 exists; instead, we have a ruling 10. Some numerologists insist on the use of the ruling 1 — in fact, the Chaldean system uses the Ruling Numbers 1 to 9 inclusive, avoiding the use of doubled numbers. The Pythagorean system exhibits greater awareness, recognising that, as 1 is the only absolute number (all others being relative to it and deriving from it) and as the Ruling Numbers are really the cardinal and most influential numbers in a person's makeup, we must recognise the 1 as being not a Ruling Number but a symbol of unity, of perfection, of the absolute. Therefore, birthdates which total 19 or 28 or 37 or 46 are classified as Ruling Number 10.

Two other special Ruling Numbers which are unique to the Pythagorean system are 11 and 22/4. Both have special metaphysical significances, as will become obvious when the qualities of these Ruling Numbers are analysed. The 11 is the highest spiritual number; the 22/4 is the double 11, plus the practical 4, making it a truly masterful combination. The 22 is found to have special significance in many different metaphysical systems and practices. It represents the highest of the major trumps in the Tarot system and is highly regarded by the gypsies as being of vital importance in human affairs.

13

RULING NUMBER 2

Only one total of numbers in the birthdate will result in a person being a ruling 2, that is the total of 20. Totals of 29, 38, and 47 result in ruling 11s. Therefore ruling 2 is one of the two most uncommon Ruling Numbers to be encountered — ruling 22/4 is the other. This is not surprising when we consider the ruling 2's purpose and how it is intended to be achieved, demanding as it does a very special strength of character.

Purpose These people have a special ability to work with and under the guidance of dynamic leadership. They are not leaders in themselves, nor have they the desire to lead, but yet they possess a unique ability of seeking out and associating with the type of person or organisation with which their own diligent capabilities may be most appreciated. Their special role is to complement by providing loyal support.

Best Expression Although extremely capable and confident when allowed to work at their own steady pace, these people can be made feel a little insecure if pushed too much. They must be allowed to progress at their own normal rate, so that they can consolidate as they go. They are exceptionally honourable and do not like their integrity being doubted — this, too, would undermine their confidence. Their best expression is generally through the use of their hands in detailed manual work, art or writing.

Distinctive Traits They are intuitive, sensitive, reliable, diligent and compassionate, possessing the important ability of peacemaker, sometimes to the extent of reforming (and in this emerging new age, this is a very valuable virtue). They are less motivated by ego than most people, possessing the selfless and noble ability of merging their ego with that of their associate, when desirable.

Negative Tendencies to be Surmounted Some fail to realise that their development must come through personal involvement, meaning work (karma yoga). Materialism or a false egocentricity will induce them to become discontented, irritable and frustrated. But these characteristics are rare, as well as being unnatural to them. In the event of such a situation occurring they will eventually recognise a departure from their Path of natural development.

Recommended Development These people should employ their intuitiveness to develop self-confidence and to choose as friends and associates those by whom their distinctive traits are best appreciated. This is important for their personal development.

As they mature, ruling 2s naturally discover the importance of emotional control — how to use it as an aid to their sensitive expression. It will be a considerable benefit to them to develop their mental faculties, especially powers of deduction and memory. Such development will firmly anchor their self-confidence.

Most Suitable Vocations   These people are suited to work as personal assistants to administrators, especially in philanthropic activities; secretaries; diplomats; social workers; process workers (if limited educational opportunities); nurses; musicians, singers or dancers with groups, but not as soloists. (It is important to note that, as we enter the next century, many more people will be born with a Ruling Number of 2. This is not surprising when we realise how much more emphasis the new age will direct towards the intuitive faculties, thereby drawing these people into a place of special significance as important guides.)

Capsule Summary   These people are supportive; intuitive; exceptionally reliable; peacemaking; compassionate; egoless; expressive through their hands.

Personality Example   Prince Philip, born June 10, 1921.
Here is an example of the classic ruling 2 person. The entire purpose of his married life is to be supportive in a minor role. Prince Philip can never become the ruler of Great Britain yet his influence is recognised as 'the power behind the throne'. In this mission he must, of necessity, be egoless and ever at the ready as peacemaker. This would prevail in his domestic life as much as in the public arena. His role as diplomat and charity organiser are also well known. Prince Philip, therefore, appears to possess all the characteristics of the ruling 2 person. His love of and participation in sports, his interest in industry and his adeptness with his hands are further attributes to complete the picture. His sensitivity is well known to all who have had close contact with Prince Philip — a trait which is also supported by the 2 on his Birthchart. Likewise, his conversational ability (supported by the three 1s on his birthchart) is eminently consistent with a ruling 2.
    When we consider that Queen Elizabeth is a ruling 7, it is apparent that her consort should be either a ruling 2 or a ruling 10. Prince Philip satisfies both requirements, as he has a 10 Day Number. This gives further strength to his power of adaptability. The desire to work as part of a team is an essential component of ruling 2 expression. In Prince Philip's life, this is evidenced domestically in his love of home and family and further supported by the combination of 6 and 9 on the Mental Plane of his Birthchart.

The life of Prince Philip, therefore, is a prime example of what a ruling 2 person can achieve, given encouragement and favourable circumstances. It should be a model by which other ruling 2 people, no matter how less fortunate in terms of worldly possessions, can fulfil their purpose.

RULING NUMBER 3

When we note its commanding position at the head of the Mental Plane (see page 43), we realise why so much emphasis is placed on thinking and on reasoning by people whose Ruling Number is 3. These are people whose birthdate numbers total 12, 21, 30, 39 or 48, each total being resolved to 3 by the addition of the component numbers.

Purpose   As these people emphasise the mental aspects of life, it is clear that their purpose relates to their thinking capabilities. For them, the understanding of life and development of personality are related to their thought processes, as opposed to intuitiveness or practical involvement. Their service to the community is similarly most beneficially expressed through thinking, planning, analysing, etc.

Best Expression   The speed with which these people engage in mental work often leaves others well behind. Their acute mental alertness is sometimes surprisingly expressed in a keen sense of humour, a natural wit which makes them very pleasant company and excellent hosts or hostesses. It must be remembered that they express themselves far better mentally than emotionally or physically.

Distinctive Traits   Their active brain, lively sense of humour and general mental alertness contribute to make ruling 3s highly successful in their working life and among their social contacts. They are often the life of the party or the brightest person in the office, but this success does not always operate in their homes. While they are socially bright and breezy, with constant companionship they often become critical. This can be very wearing on close associates, especially on the spouse. They enjoy helping people, so long as they have rapport on a mental level and the other people are prepared to be co-operative.

Negative Tendencies to be Surmounted   When not living constructively, these people may assume an unpleasant air of superiority and this can create many misunderstandings. Being so alert mentally, negative ruling 3s manifest a lack of patience and tolerance of others less blessed, becoming quite critical of their 'limitations'. This fault finding is invariably carried into their homes, often involving them in broken marriages and/or family ties. In some instances, this constant criticism can become such a heavy burden upon the spouse that it will lead to his or her shortened life span.

Recommended Development
These people must learn to develop a sensitivity to the feelings of others. In recognising that life's experiences are a constant school of learning, their graduation rate is greatly improved when they learn to live in harmony. This makes for a more positive outlook on life. Ruling 3 people must learn not to blame others but to use their natural power of resilience to bounce back with renewed vigour, looking upon the experience as a helpful opportunity. It will be of great benefit to them to broaden their base of expression, by cultivating their intuitiveness and by being more practical in day to day affairs, especially around the home; e.g., by actually cutting the lawn rather than theorising about how it should be done.

Most Suitable Vocations
By nature they are suited to work as welfare workers; social organisers; research scientists and physicians (but not in general practice); artists, writers and actors in the field of light entertainment; critics; academics; analysts; accountants and businessmen.

Capsule Summary
These people are assessing; mentally alert; planning; analytic; with sense of humour; often with marriage problems.

Personality Example
Don Dunstan, born September 21, 1926.

The nature of the ruling 3 person is typified by Don Dunstan — indeed, it is magnified by the fact that he is also a 3 Day Number. He is very much a thinking person, is critical and assertive, with a lively sense of humour and a great love of acting. Now that he is free of political commitments, we will see Don Dunstan become more and more involved in acting and the world of entertainment. In this he will be very successful, so long as he allows his expression to flow freely and does not become unduly self-critical.

His domestic life has been far from happy, involving him in a more-than-average share of responsibilities (the 6 and double 9 on his Birthchart). But the rationalising ability of the ruling 3 has stood firmly by him, giving him reasons for occurrences, explanations which are vital to his peace of mind and his ability to organise his life accordingly. Significant changes in lifestyle are certainly not uncharacteristic of a ruling 3 person.

To many people, Don Dunstan appears to assume an air of

superiority and judgement. This is not an impression he intends to convey, but rather is one which develops with most ruling 3 people. They tend to become too prone to assess people, including themselves. In Don Dunstan's case, this can often reveal itself as impatience with people who are mentally slow at grasping concepts he seeks to convey (exacerbated by the lack of 4 on his Birthchart).

Don Dunstan typifies the ruling 3 person in his varying moods, oscillating between bright humour and deep contemplation and assessment. These people would find a far greater level of personal happiness were they to learn to relax more mentally, and to also allow others the freedom to be themselves — without excuse or justification.

RULING NUMBER 4

In this modern world, where so much general emphasis is placed on material concerns, the basic expression of most people with a Ruling Number 4 can be easily gratified. But there is more to them than materialism, although their major emphasis certainly lies on the physical, 4 being located on the centre of the Practical Plane. Birthdates whose component numbers total 13, 31, 40 or 49 have Ruling Numbers of 4.

Purpose While we are incarnated on the Earth Plane, human experience is usually related to the material. This is especially so with ruling 4 people, whose development in early life is to recognise how well they express at this level. But as these people mature they find their purpose elevates to more of an organisational one, thereby allowing for greater scope in gaining awareness and wisdom.

Best Expression A wide range of expression can apply to these people, encompassing most physical and organisational work. It can range from the pleasure of making money for its own sake, through the artistic aspects of repairing and renovating objects or art pieces, to the organisation of extensive sporting, business or cultural affairs. In whatever they do, ruling 4s are generally quite orthodox, rarely evidencing any wish to be different.

Distinctive Traits These are people with a natural flair for using their hands, and often their feet. Their love of practicality keeps ruling 4s on the go. They can rarely sit still and see others do the organising, invariably coming forward to offer worthwhile assistance. They are among the most systematic, reliable and trustworthy of people. This is especially evident in detailed work, where their accuracy and practical ability are second to none.

Negative Tendencies to be Surmounted
Dependent upon their emotional makeup, these individuals will either become totally absorbed in their work and their responsibilities or will lose heart due to frustrated ambition. More frequently the former prevails, and when it does, care must be taken that they do not neglect their domestic or social lives. Should they become so neglectful, a hard, materialistic outlook can easily develop. This can lead to emotional unhappiness and greatly inhibit the development of their purpose in life.

Recommended Development
Three important avenues of development should be undertaken by ruling 4s — relaxation, mental application, expanded intuitiveness. Relaxation is important as a means of detachment from material concerns and from physical involvements; it also provides an excellent basis for mental and spiritual development. Such relaxation is best achieved through meditation techniques which direct thought into channels of concentration and then relaxation. The most suitable forms of mental application are in memory training and the employment of academic principles related to manual skills (engineering, for example). Seeking the principles behind outward manifestations will assist with expanded intuitiveness. This can also be achieved through practical involvement (doing it yourself) in music and art, as well as through the study of the science of numbers.

Most Suitable Vocations
These people are suited to work as skilled tradesmen; technicians; craftsmen; managers of commercial concerns; economists, but not in an advisory capacity as they do not usually possess sufficiently sound judgement; authors of technical books or magazines; horticulturists; physicians; chiropractors.

Capsule Summary
These people are practical; organising; orthodox in outlook; often materialistic; interested in sports, very capable with their hands.

Personality Example
Kerry Packer, born December 17, 1937.

Few people who know him would deny that Kerry Packer is a 'workaholic'. A highly capable organiser, a practical man, a sportsman with a materialistic outlook, Kerry Packer combines these attributes to achieve a unique level of success in his fields of endeavour. These exemplify the positive aspects of the ruling 4 person.

Nobody has shaken the world of cricket, throughout its long history, more than has Kerry Packer. Although his actions are somewhat unorthodox from the viewpoint of cricket tradition, they are not inconsistent with the nature of a ruling 4 person who channels his sporting interests and organising ability into a combined effort, navigated towards a financial goal. By so doing, he has introduced established business practice into one of the few sporting domains which, hitherto, was comparatively immune from commercial contamination.

But the achievements of Kerry Packer have needed more than the abilities implied by the ruling 4 per se because they are obviously the work of a highly capable planner. His planning and mental balance are recognised in his Birthchart, where we see the Arrow of the Planner and the balanced Mental Plane. These combine to make for a powerful force which, in Packer's case, could result in a hard, materialistic outlook if he did not take care to control it, rather than letting it control him. Such materialism would, in turn, breed emotional discontent in his personal life, driving him more acutely along the avenue in which he knows he excels — work. He must learn to introduce balance into his activities if he is to find total satisfaction and happiness.

RULING NUMBER 5

In practice we find that people with the Ruling Number 5 invariably strive to be free of confinement. This is a natural expression of their highly sensitive nature. It is not surprising when we realise that 5 is the centre of the Spiritual Plane and of the Arrow of the Will. Those birthdates whose component numbers total 14, 23, 32, or 41 have a Ruling Number of 5.

Purpose   The mastery of sensitive expression (whether through verse, prose, painting or sculpture, etc.) is one of the real refinements of all human life. However, it can only be achieved when adequate freedom prevails. It is just this type of expression which ruling 5 people seek to develop as a means of acquiring the command and understanding of their emotions. But few of them are aware of this, feeling only the drive for freedom, ignorant of its real reason which is to learn to constructively direct their lives by means of it.

Best Expression   Many of these people find difficulty in working for a boss. They should seek a job which allows them to work without immediate direction, such as that of a travelling salesman, freelance writer or reporter. By this means they will enjoy a much-needed freedom to develop their most suitable avenue of expression. A strong desire for adventure is often felt by them. Indeed, this urge to travel and experience can be a valuable means of attaining needed freedom and enlightenment. A further avenue in which they can happily express their feelings is entertaining (both in the home and on the stage).

Distinctive Traits

They are intuitive people, with a strong artistic flair, gaining immeasurable pleasure from being free to express themselves. With such freedom they are lively and dynamic; but if confined they tend to become sullen and apathetic. Yet they are usually very goodnatured people with a strong determination to enjoy life and to help others do so as well.

Negative Tendencies to be Surmounted

This strong love of freedom can sometimes drive ruling 5s to the employment of illegal activities to avoid being confined to a job. They thereby fail to recognise the purpose of such temporary confinement: to learn the lessons they need in patience, co-operation and self-control. Many young ruling 5s, taking a job for the first time, rebel at having to answer to a boss and decide to take unemployment benefits — in fact, statistics prove there are significantly more ruling 5 people out of work than people of any other Ruling Number. When inattentive to detail, ruling 5s make poor businessmen and should not get themselves deeply involved in commerce. This is further emphasised by their tendency towards nervousness and uncertainty when confined to the workaday world. Such nervousness can lead to irritability and eventually to depression if not controlled. Care should be taken to restore calmness by spending more time with nature.

Recommended Development

Very often man's search for freedom is a hankering for those pristine days of carefree innocence, the recollections of which are occasionally stimulated to bring to our consciousness a glimpse of many incarnations passed. But we cannot live in history, except to use its lessons for our further development. Thus, when current circumstances appear to restrict us we should be aware of the lessons we are intended to derive from them. Then we can move on, graduating away from such confinement. There is need for ruling 5 people to develop more attention to detail, for in this manner they gain a wider perspective of life through greater practicality. They should accept suitable opportunities for travel to develop their powers of observation as a means of understanding more about life.

Most Suitable Vocations

These people are suited to work as salespeople; travel consultants; actors; writers; theatrical directors or producers; designers or inventors; politicians; social workers and reformers.

Capsule Summary   Their nature is independent; intuitive; artistic; adventurous; moody — oscillating between joviality when free to be emotionally expressive, and sullenness when feeling suppressed.

Personality Example   Caroline Jones, born January 1, 1938. Well known for her radio and television interviewing, Caroline Jones excels in the application of her sensitivity to the personality of her interviewee. She intuitively knows how to encourage people to be openly expressive, drawing them into the atmosphere which makes for an interesting interview. She can only achieve this by being allowed considerable freedom in the preparation of her material.

Were she to be under the direction of a suppressive boss, Caroline Jones would suffer from emotional discontent. With the freedom to express her own natural talents, we see only her strong artistic flair and her jovial good nature, free of the frustrations and impatience which would otherwise become apparent. Impatience was an aspect of her earlier life which she had to learn to overcome — and this she appears to have achieved rather well. However, she is not yet free of the frustrations associated with disappointment in people, especially some close friends who, over the years, have let her down or have tried to override her personality with their own.

As her maturity blossoms Caroline Jones will become more creative, most probably through writing or painting. She will discover that such avenues of creative expression provide her with a satisfaction hitherto unrecognised by her soul. But she must realise that such growth is slow, opening to full beauty only under the guidance of natural development through personal self-control.

RULING NUMBER 6

This is a Ruling Number of extremes. These people have the potential for great creative power when living positively; but when living negatively, they become incessant worriers. The position of this number in the centre of the Mental Plane and at the head of the Will Arrow gives ruling 6 people tremendous potential to perceive and create brilliantly. Regrettably, they rarely achieve such levels in practice. Birthdates with component numbers totalling 15, 24, 33 or 42 have a Ruling Number of 6.

Purpose   Here we find people who excel as creative artists, dramatists, or, on the more private level, as exemplary homemakers and comforters to mankind. This implies a very important responsibility in human affairs, one which demands a deep, loving dedication. All people with this Ruling Number possess such capacity, but often they become so physically identified with their responsibilities that anxiety and emotional worries entrap them. Ruling 6 people must learn to master those situations into which their great capacities for love and creativity draw them, rather than let the situations control them. To this end, they must learn the art of loving detachment so that they may express their beautiful creativity, yet not be imposed upon.

Best Expression   These people excel in positions or situations in which their trust, creativity and deep sense of responsibility are called for. Some prefer to express these talents publicly, excelling in dramatic stagecraft as actors or singers. At the core of their expression is always that deep love of humanity and a loving, goodnature which is a joy to share.

Distinctive Traits   Their exceptional creativity finds every opportunity to express itself at work, pleasure and in the home. To ruling 6 people the home is the most important place; it occupies a considerable amount of their creativity and is second in importance only to their loved ones within it. Being great humanitarians, these people resent injustices of any kind and are exceptionally loving, unselfish and tolerant.

Negative Tendencies to be Surmounted   When opportunities for expressing their creativity are limited to the home (as is the case with so many housewives of this Ruling Number), overemphasis towards the home as being their castle can create an unbalanced and unhealthy possessiveness. These feelings can be equally as strong towards the family, especially the children, to the extent that extreme worry and overanxiety will develop. This leads to all sorts of apprehensions, fears, caution and constriction such that personal development is severely thwarted. Worry often becomes so chronic as to result in mild psychosis, bringing with it a sad loneliness which is totally the opposite of everything they were endeavouring to create. When worry and negativeness prevail in the lives of ruling 6s, they adopt a whining voice and take on the air of a fault finder. They must remember that a positive mental outlook is of utmost importance to the development of creativity, whatever the physical limitations.

Recommended Development   Let those with this Ruling Number learn that love is a state of being, of freedom — not of possession. Possession is foreign to love, often destroying love as it produces restrictions and anxiety. Love is a state of joyousness and is above emotional limitations, yet it can call upon emotional expression to indicate its presence — but no more than indicate.

Love should not be confused with, or limited by, the emotions, any more than the celebration of Christmas should be limited to the giving of gifts. Ruling 6 people must learn to develop a wise firmness. This will not hamper their creative development but rather permit it, for it will ensure they are not imposed upon by unthinking or selfish people.

Most Suitable Vocations
Whatever they do must have creative prospects and, therefore must directly or ultimately be for the betterment of human welfare. They excel as social workers; managers of humanitarian organisations and healers of people or animals. They can also become excellent dramatic artists.

Capsule Summary
These people are creative; loving; just; unselfish; tolerant; homeloving; but inclined towards deep worry and extreme anxiety.

Personality Example
Bob Hawke, born December 9, 1929. Few people would deny that Bob Hawke is a just and unselfish man when involved in championing the rights of those whom he has chosen to represent. He is deeply resentful of injustice, which draws from him a viciousness in his attempts to destroy its influence. This is the creativity of the ruling 6 being applied in reverse — destructiveness.

He is happiest when involved in creative activities, exemplified in his efforts to develop better working conditions and more equitable rewards when he feels the prevailing ones are inadequate. But he is tolerant of other points of view, wherein lies his special power as a negotiator.

Although Bob Hawke is sometimes misrepresented by the media when they attempt to portray him as a volatile, tempestuous hardhead, an impulsive idealism is so entrenched in his personality (indicated by the three 9s on his Birthchart) that all his creative efforts must be directed towards the common good, as he sees it. This will often create the illusion of fanaticism.

There is no doubt that Bob Hawke is a worrier. His furrowed brow attests to this, yet he attempts to allay any outward suspicion of worry in his demeanour. He is easily inclined towards such depth of concern when he feels injustice is being perpetrated that he will worry about the situation until he can organise to have it reversed. This tendency will militate against the success of his proposed entry into federal parliament, for there he will find circumstances far too complex and too cumbersome for him to exercise as much control as he would want. In short, his health could be significantly impaired if he proceeds with his expressed intention of gaining recognition as a parliamentarian unless he undertakes a programme designed to train him in controlled relaxation and emotional containment.

Bob Hawke's opponents should never underestimate his intuitive ability. He has a very profound sense of knowing things in advance of their expression and of assessing situations before they develop (two 2s on his Birthchart). He will, however, experience many more frustrations in his personal life, especially with regard to friendships, where some in whom he has placed his trust will betray him (indicated by the Arrow of Frustrations: no 4-5-6). This has to be carefully controlled, for it would otherwise exacerbate his tendency to worry, precipitating any number of nerve-oriented health disorders.

RULING NUMBER 7

This is the Ruling Number under which people gain maximum experience, both through learning and through teaching (teaching being the consummate means of learning). Both facets of growth are, of course, intimately related to physical expression, symbolised by the position of the 7 on the Birthchart at the intersection of the Practical Plane and the Activity Arrow (see pages 43 and 88).

Purpose   It would appear that the manner by which individual human development takes place in life ensures that each soul incarnates with a Ruling Number 7 when it is necessary to undertake a major step forward. The unique aspect of this Ruling Number is its almost limitless capacity for learning through personal involvement. Enlightenment gained in such a way invariably qualifies ruling 7 people to be able to share their experiences, making them excellent teachers.

Best Expression   One of the most important requirements in these people's lives is that they be allowed to learn their way. They can accept only a minimum of direction from others, as they hunger to learn by personal involvement and expression: the involvement demands sacrifices of them; the expression of their acquired knowledge manifests itself in teaching, for they are devoted helpers of mankind. Ruling 7 people find someone else's discipline very difficult to live with, yet develop their own self-imposed programme by which their lives are directed — and by which they sometimes like to direct other people's lives.

Distinctive Traits   These people are found among the most active in all walks of life. Although not always conscious of it, their driving force is the need for personal experience. It is a fundamental law of human life that personal experiences become the most memorable, consequently the most valuable, when they are the result of personal sacrifices. This is the Path of the Ruling Number 7. Many of them appear to have rather sad lives, suffering losses in love, money or health when their actions are in conflict with their higher guidance. But they possess a tremendous natural fortitude as well as an inherent confidence and deep philosophical understanding, recognising that everything occurs for a purpose.

Negative Tendencies to be Surmounted
Their compulsion for personal experience, to the point of rejecting guidance, will sometimes cause ruling 7s to become extremely rebellious. In refusing to accept advice, they adopt the attitude of 'I like learning, but I do not like being taught'. This can lead them into all sorts of seemingly unnecessary sadnesses as they fail to learn by an intelligent application of advice. Yet they often endeavour to enjoin other people to follow their advice and become annoyed if they get the same response to advice as they give to others. Until they mature and act more wisely, their domestic and business lives will be far from happy; in fact, they should avoid financial involvement in business, as they rarely possess a sound understanding of economics.

Recommended Development
It would be of great benefit to ruling 7s if they embraced as much discipline in their lives as they seek to teach others. By this means, they will evolve a more reliable intuition and a well-balanced philosophical outlook. They are naturally slow learners, due to their need to experience so much for themselves. Parents should take special note of this characteristic and permit their ruling 7 children to learn at their own speed. All too often parents regard their children's progress at school as some sort of prestige race, acting as though they are more concerned with the family name than with the children's welfare. The family must realise that children with this Ruling Number learn rapidly until age seven, at which time they seem to need to stabilise. Their academic learning rate decreases markedly between ages seven and fourteen — a very important period of spiritual growth in their lives when they turn inward for the first time. From age fourteen onwards their academic learning rate will increase once more, but rarely do these children emerge as brilliant scholars.

Most Suitable Vocations
Being very trustworthy themselves and consequently expecting trust from others, these people are ideally suited to positions among the judiciary and in legal practice. They are also people who are adept at the use of

sharp instruments. Many therefore choose careers as surgeons, butchers, carpenters. As one would expect, many teachers are found among ruling 7 people, as are clergy, technicians, scientists, naturalists and philosophers.

Capsule Summary   Needing to learn by personal experience; disliking discipline; assertive; philosophical; teaching and helpful; leading a life in which many sacrifices must be experienced.

Personality Example   Sir Winston Churchill, born November 30, 1874.

'I like to learn but I do not want to be taught'. It is unknown whether Sir Winston Churchill used this exact expression but he certainly epitomised its meaning in his general attitude towards people. He was indeed a typical ruling 7, in that he regarded life as a series of personal learning experiences. But he had to learn by his own involvement.

The earlier life of Sir Winston Churchill was highlighted by some brilliant decisions; and others which were not quite so worthy of his ability. He was very much a self-disciplined man and it is obvious from his Ruling Number that he did not take kindly to externally imposed rules and regulations. As he matured, his fierce non-disciplinarian manner would have mellowed to enable him to gain more guidance from the experienced advisors available to a man in such a high position.

That he was assertive and had a deep philosophical basis to his attitudes and actions are characteristics well recorded. When we recognise that on his Birthchart his greatest strength lies on the Practical Plane (with the Arrow of Practicality), we understand how he was able to achieve so much over an extensive span of years.

It is not uncommon for ruling 7 people to be aggressive if they feel that others are imposing their will on them or if they sense that their freedom is being restricted. Such aggressiveness was a characteristic of the young Winston Churchill whose pugnaciousness was a defence to protect his highly sensitive nature.

It was not until his later years his intuition developed sufficiently to enable him to discriminate wisely in his selection of associates and acquaintances. Ruling 7 people are often quite slow in learning how to deal with people in their earlier years and, especially without a 2 on his Birthchart, Sir Winston Churchill had to develop such knowledge by the control of his temper and by careful observation. To learn in this manner is necessary to most people, but especially to ruling 7s.

RULING NUMBER 8

These are people who regard independence as one of the most important aspects of life. They can be very complex people who invariably possess great strength of character. Their power derives from the position of the 8 on the Spiritual (feeling) Plane, as well as being in the centre of the Arrow of Activity. Ruling Number 8 birthdates are those which total 17, 26, 35 or 44.

Purpose   One of the most important aspects of love is our ability to express it. One of the most important components of successful human relationships is a fluent ability to express appreciation (itself, a vital embodiment of love). It is in these two avenues of expression that Ruling Number 8 people find greatest difficulty; consequently, an essential feature of their purpose in life is to transcend these limitations. Growth in this direction comes with the realisation that, rather than inhibiting their independence, such improved relationships strengthen the confidence others have in them. This, in turn, creates greater personal security and improved happiness in their lives.

Best Expression   Seemingly inconsistent for Ruling Number 8s is their enormous capacity for compassion and sympathetic tenderness for those in trouble. However, not always do they express themselves in this way for long, tending to grow impatient with those who become dependent upon them, for this hampers their own independence. They are generally most successful in business, particularly if they can express their abilities freely without emotional misunderstandings. Ruling 8 people are generally very conscious of how they dress, taking great pride in their appearance.

Distinctive Traits   A strong air of independence and dependability, together with a self-confident manner, are distinctive in the attitudes of the ruling 8. Both qualities work in harmony to equip them for positions of seniority and responsibility in which many are found in industry and commerce. But their independence transmutes to an undemonstrative attitude of coolness, bordering on indifference, in the home. This is related to their difficulties of self-expression, inhibitions which maturity often helps to overcome. Their expressed love for helpless creatures — for animals, infants, the dependent and the very sick — is constantly seeking to be expressed.

Negative Tendencies to be Surmounted   Their fierce independence is often so zealously guarded that these people develop a deep resentment toward any form of (what they regard as) interference in their plans. Therefore great diplomacy and tact must be employed by those seeking to guide them. Indeed, ruling 8 people need a good deal of guidance, especially in their handling of children, where they find difficulty in adopting the middle path — they are either overindulgent or exceptionally strict.

Recommended Development
Every effort should be made to overcome the undemonstrativeness which they unvaryingly exhibit towards their loved ones. Until this is achieved they will not find real happiness in the home. They must learn to eschew aloofness and to express overtly the appreciation and love they possess for their spouse, rather than hide these feelings and expect the spouse to know they exist. A successful marriage cannot be achieved when one partner takes the other for granted.

Most Suitable Vocations
These people are suited to work as senior executives in commerce and industry; bankers and financiers; stockbrokers and investors; philanthropists; travel executives; aircraft and ship's captains; teachers and nurses to children; animal welfare workers; zookeepers and animal trainers.

Capsule Summary
These people are independent; dependable; self-confident; undemonstrative; commercially oriented; deeply concerned for the sick and the helpless.

Personality Example
Johannes Bjelke-Petersen, born January 13, 1911.

To describe him as independent, confident and commercially oriented would satisfy some of the impressions given by the present premier of Queensland. However, to a majority of Australians, he appears as arrogant and terse, with a self-confidence which is more a mask than a reality.

Few would think of Joh Bjelke-Petersen as shy, yet it is this deep, personal sensitivity which caused him to develop an inferiority complex as a youngster and which now tends to make him over-react when challenged on issues which he regards as personal or involving his personal judgement. In so doing he often misrepresents his genuine concern for the social conditions he is seeking to improve.

Joh's habit of attracting unfavourable publicity derives from his many inner conflicts. He holds himself aloof, not only as a means of protecting himself from those who seek to intrude upon his personal life and thoughts, but also because he seeks to protect the independence he so cherishes. Bjelke-Petersen feels he is doing the best possible job as premier and expects others to believe it too. In the main, he is highly dependable, but this is often overshadowed by the apparent egocentricity of his self-confidence. We must remember that this is a very independent man who prefers demonstrating his abilities in

29

action to explaining or verbally justifying them.

When analysing a person as controversial as Joh Bjelke-Petersen, we should be careful to prevent any media or political bias from entering into our assessments. Falling into such error would obscure our recognition of some of the capabilities which have contributed to the success of this man in his businesslike guidance of his state's commercial affairs. His commercial orientation underlies his apparent inflexibility where it comes to social issues, when he feels they interfere with the financial life of his domain. Yet this is another of his inconsistencies, for he is highly sensitive to the needs of the sick, the underprivileged and the helpless — it is in these areas where he feels at ease demonstrating his empathy, for he knows he will be appreciated.

In most of his daily involvements, Joh Bjelke-Petersen's attitudes are far too reactive to attract him to many people, although some secretly respect the success he seems to have achieved in many fields. These are not uncommon reactions to the ruling 8 in public life, especially the older ruling 8s, for they do not find it easy to relate to 'new age' consciousness and sharing — Lang Hancock is a further example, although he does not have as many personality problems to overcome as has Joh.

RULING NUMBER 9

Responsibility and humanitarian concern are the two most vital aspects of this Ruling Number. These are people who put people before things, who put principle before principal. They are individuals whose birthdate numbers total 18, 27, 36 or 45.

Purpose   This is a powerful Ruling Number in the affairs of man. Those who possess it are intended to number among the guardians of our cultural heritage. They are far more suited to art than to science, to humanitarian rather than to commercial pursuits. Most of our potential philosophers, reformers and cultural leaders are to be found with this Ruling Number, although not always are their idealistic concepts the most workable — it is an important aspect of their purpose in life to learn to translate the idealistic into the practical.

Best Expression   The serving of humanity and the improving of earthly life are at the heart of the ruling 9's expression. The method by which they can best achieve this will be indicated by the formation and analysis of their Birthchart. These people are ambitious for the principles they revere, but are inclined to be more concerned with the overall plan than with its details. Therefore they should concentrate upon non-commercial undertakings — indeed they are poor financial managers. They are very artistic, preferring the deeply serious to the comic or popular forms of artistic expression.

Distinctive Traits
Responsibility is their forte; they are exceptionally honest and intensely idealistic. Honesty is so natural to them that they assume everyone to be so inclined. This often leads to great disappointments in people. They would rather give money to needy people than save it for themselves. They have very definite thoughts about life and its ideals, about humanity and how people should be motivated. Even though these ideas are not always the most practical, ruling 9s will always strive to implement them, for in these areas they are ambitious people.

Negative Tendencies to be Surmounted
An indication of negative living is when these people fail to adopt the ideals they seek to impress on others. Great care has to be taken to ensure that they do not fall victim to one of the most offensive of all human transgressions — hypocrisy. Their ambitions can dominate and destroy the integrity of their ideals, thereby developing an egocentricity which is far from appealing. This will often produce a very abrupt manner and an attitude of destructive criticism which their associates will find difficult to tolerate.

Recommended Development
The strong idealism of the ruling 9 does not make for good judges of character. Yet once this limitation is realised it can be remedied by their studying a reliable guide to understanding people, such as the science of numbers. Such a study will help them to investigate all aspects of a person before drawing conclusions. This, in turn, will help develop intuition. Patience and persistence are two other important traits which these people often lack but which can be cultivated from the numerological study of their own and other people's personalities.

Most Suitable Vocations
These people are suited to work as religious ministers; reformers; philanthropists; organisers of humanitarian projects; conciliators; researchers; criminologists; healers; archaeologists; actors; painters, writers or sculptors of an intensely serious nature.

Capsule Summary
Ruling 9s are responsible; extremely honest; idealistic; ambitious; humanitarian; very poor at saving money; with a serious attitude to life.

Personality Example
Joan Sutherland, born November 7, 1926.

There has probably never been a more powerful or richer

soprano voice to grace the stages of the world's opera houses than that belonging to Australia's Joan Sutherland. The combination of her musical and acting talents has guaranteed her a unique place in the musical history books; but it is only fair to say that she could never have achieved such success on her own.

Possessing the idealism, honesty and seriousness characteristic of a ruling 9 person, Joan Sutherland must have always combined these with a ceaseless ambition to reach the top. Yet for so many years she appeared unable to make it. This situation illustrates the typical traits of ruling 9s, together with their affinity for the tragic, so in evidence in Joan Sutherland's most famous role as Lucia di Lammermoor, a role which was instrumental in bringing her worldwide accolades.

However, these qualities were insufficient in themselves. A very necessary driving force was absent, as seems to be the case with many ruling 9 people. This inherent insufficiency is further indicated by the lack of any arrows on the Birthchart (see Stage 7). Certainly, her name gave some assistance, but insufficient for her to travel such an arduous path as was necessary to reach the top of her chosen profession without the guidance of a dynamic manager.

The entry of Richard Bonynge into her life brought to Joan Sutherland every quality necessary for her to succeed. His unique attributes were ideally supplementary to hers — his creative idealism and vast wealth of knowledge have been her godsend. However, she must take care that, in this relationship, he does not deprive her of the satisfaction she must derive from the acceptance of deep personal responsibility. Creative genius can unthinkingly assume such total command that no room remains for others to exercise their special talents. Joan Sutherland must recognise her abilities and choose her roles accordingly — this responsibility is important to her personal satisfaction. All the same, she is not a good judge of character and is often quite gullible — indicating the area in which she will always need the astute guidance of one who is not a ruling 9.

RULING NUMBER 10

Most Ruling Numbers can be expressed in a variety of ways, depending on the degree of awareness of the person. But there is probably no greater range of expression than that found in people with the Ruling Number 10. They vary from most likeable, personality plus people when living positively, to lost, floundering, insecure people, when existing negatively. However, they are essentially the most adaptable of people which favours them with an excellent ability to adjust to life's contingencies. The Ruling Number 10 applies to birthdates which have number totals of 19, 28, 37 or 46.

Purpose

Ruling 10 people have incarnated with two prime purposes — to learn to readily adjust to life's many vicissitudes, and to help others to adjust. As life becomes more complex, human adaptation becomes the more vital. Yet to the Ruling Number 10, the adjustment presents no problem. This quality greatly facilitates their helping others, both in mediating between people and in assisting them to harmonise with external circumstances.

Best Expression

If ever we are looking for somebody to help us enjoy the light-hearted pleasures of life, we would generally find no better person than a ruling 10. They express best when allowed the freedom of what they regard as the bubbling excitement of life. But when they are suppressed or feel emotionally hampered, they become most despondent without realising why. It is as though the joy of their expression has been lost forever and this gives rise to much frustration in their dealings with people, especially evident by short temper and irritability. The minority of ruling 10 people who have discovered the true depth to their personality and the real meaning of their life, will recognise it and are not so reactive — although they will find they are not as light-hearted as those just described, they are invariably consistently optimistic in their approach to life, expressed through a buoyant personality.

Distinctive Traits

Their innate power of adaptability to people and circumstances makes ruling 10s popular in almost every walk of life. They possess a natural ability for making people happy although — because they prefer not to delve too deeply into other people's problems — they do not always realise why others lapse into disharmony. In fact, they do not delve deeply into their own lives, contenting themselves more with the pleasures of the moment, while their air of self-assurance can easily mislead others into thinking they have total command of themselves. This self-assurance is usually based on their physical and social aptitudes (such as in sports and at parties), noticeably diminishing where emotional involvements are concerned. In a lighthearted manner, they are artistic in expression, with a sensitive touch which makes them good instrumentalists and capable judges of quality in clothing and materials.

Negative Tendencies to be Surmounted

Their self-confidence can sometimes lead these people to dominate others, but they dominate unwisely, invariably creating instead of overcoming disharmony. This tendency is best avoided by keeping the ego under control. When not engaged in creative or constructive activities for any significant period ruling 10s tend to lapse into superficiality, expecting life to be just one big ball, complaining if things do not go well for them, but doing little to improve themselves. Unless they are surrounded by bright company, they can easily become melancholy and emotionally insecure. They must be taught to practise the most reliable means of finding themselves and of achieving inner peace — the discovery of silence through meditation.

Recommended Development
The most important aim for a ruling 10 is training to strengthen their individuality. They must not allow themselves to get lost in conformity or mediocrity but, rather, expand their powers of awareness by a conscious application of discipline and self-expression. To everyone, the Pythagorean disciplines are indispensable exercises in self-enlightenment; to a ruling 10, they are doubly beneficial. Based on silence and meditation, these exercises cover such essentials as memory training, moderation, fortitude, compassion, harmony and order.

Most Suitable Vocations
These people are suited to work as interior decorators and designers; buyers of fabrics and materials; salespeople; politicians of the loyal party type, but not statesmen; town planners and architects; light entertainers; professional sportspeople; charity fundraisers.

Capsule Summary
The ruling 10 is confident; debonair; bright, with a general happy disposition; possesses an extremely sensitive touch; very capable in buying and selling.

Personality Example
Rupert Murdoch, born March 11, 1931.

Very few Australians have made their mark on the competitive world of international commerce to the same degree as has Rupert Murdoch. His ventures into the hallowed portals of Fleet Street and the corporate publishing world of New York City astounded even the most hardened media executives around the world. But Rupert Murdoch was not to be intimidated.

Skill in buying and selling, his debonair and sensitive attitude, his abundant self-confidence, and his ready adaptability have combined to make Rupert Murdoch an example of the heights to which a ruling 10 person can aspire. Most ruling 10 people are inclined to be happy-go-lucky, content to be average, popular people who enjoy a good time, but who never appear to achieve much in life. Yet, when they recognise their latent abilities, ruling 10s can become dynamic individuals, especially in activities where skills in buying and selling and where personal persuasiveness are demanded, for here they excel.

Life has not always been a pattern of success for Rupert Murdoch. Nor will it always be one. But his adaptability will always stand by him, allowing him to exercise exceptional flexibility. If he attempts a business proposition which eventually turns sour he will not stubbornly persist against the impossible, but will about-face and develop a different approach or even undertake an entirely new venture.

Murdoch's acute mental alertness has its roots in the two 3s on his Birthchart. These also significantly contribute to his literary ability, but he must take care that he does not become so mentally hyperactive that he fails to relax. If he would learn to meditate, his mental abilities would have a far longer life expectancy and he would maintain a better balance in his attitude towards other people. Because of his hypersensitivity, Rupert Murdoch occasionally over-reacts to the two extremes of people — those who appear to challenge him and those who are mentally lazy. Tolerance is an important factor in his success in relating to people and will help to attract cheery people about him, their presence being a necessary palliative to melancholy and emotional insecurity.

RULING NUMBER 11

An especially high level of spirituality surrounds this Ruling Number, offering those born to it a unique potential for the development of their intuition, clairvoyance and similar metaphysical faculties. Unfortunately, more people fail to live up to this potential power than develop it, but this pattern is changing with the approach of the new age of awareness. In practice, we do not find so many ruling 11s, for only two birthdate totals currently qualify — 29 and 38.

Purpose These people are among the few who are potentially best equipped to guide mankind into the emerging new age. It is a very responsible incarnation they have chosen. Unfortunately, many find that as life's physical attractions become recognised by them they are diverted from their higher purpose. As man moves into the new age he is becoming aware of those profound metaphysical forces which express themselves through the faculties of clairvoyance, intuition, E.S.P., psychometry, spiritual healing, etc. A high proportion of ruling 11 people will be found forging ahead in the developments in this field.

Best Expression As lovers of refinement, beauty and the cultural virtues of life, people with this Ruling Number gravitate towards such an environment because it liberates them to express their innate spirituality. Material life, for them, is demanding and uninteresting, but they have to learn to balance it with the ideal they seek within. That is why we are here on Earth Plane; for the noblest of spiritual virtues is of little value unless it can be transmitted into practical application, unless it can be employed to improve the quality of life. No finer expression can be found than in doing this.

Distinctive Traits   There are extreme differences between the lifestyles of the ruling 11 who lives positively and utilises his exceptional spiritual powers and his negative counterpart whose life appears difficult and colourless. An uncompromisingly high level of morality, profoundly reliable intuitiveness and inspired driving force are clearly in evidence when these people are involved in spiritually oriented pursuits. They are extremely dependable, honest and just, with a deep love for family and friends, together with a sincere compassion for all life.

Negative Tendencies to be Surmounted   Temptation to abdicate our responsibility for virtuous living becomes stronger as modern commercialism seeks new and more devious ways to sell its overproduction of often unnecessary commodities. Life is meant to be far less complicated, far more harmonious than many people now find it. Such complexities can easily confuse and misdirect sensitive people from their Path. When this happens they can become bitter and spiteful, often indifferent in their attitude toward other people and to their work. Special efforts should be made by ruling 11s to avoid these pitfalls and elevate themselves above the enticement of material wants, recognising how foreign those wants are to their own real needs or the needs of others. This step will demand more than average effort of will. It might even alienate them from other materially motivated people.

Recommended Development   Spiritual faculties do not mix well with commerce for the ruling 11. Consequently, their best avenues for development lie in those professions which can facilitate growth in spiritual awareness, as well as providing adequate monetary rewards. Their natural generosity and spontaneous habits of assisting people in need — admirable virtues, indeed — create a more-than-average demand on the financial resources of ruling 11s, so they should learn to recognise priorities and be guided by their intuition, rather than any desires for recognition. They are often tempted to reject assistance for themselves when in need, but must learn to be more receptive and recognise the benefits which can accrue to the giver and receiver of such practical co-operation.

Most Suitable Vocations   Ruling 11 people often excel as educationists; social workers; religious or art teachers; architects;

explorers; geologists; designers or inventors; artistic performers (so long as there is an underlying moral value). It is important to realise that ruling 11s rarely succeed in business, although they have a great capacity for supporting any business in which the common good is served.

Capsule Summary   These people are highly sensitive; love refinement, beauty and all things which have a deep cultural substance; intensely honest and compassionate, often preferring to avoid the life of hard business.

Personality Example   Wolfgang Mozart, born January 27, 1756.

Any visitor to the quaint Austrian city of Salzburg could not help but feel saddened that the most famous citizen of that city should die in such abject poverty after enriching the world with the most beautiful of musical compositions. No composer has ever rivalled Mozart for the sheer brilliance, beauty and diversity of his musical genius. Even so, many contemporaries patterned their developing styles on his (the great Beethoven being no exception, for his First Symphony is almost Mozartian), recognising in Mozart a depth of spiritual beauty which captured their very souls.

No lover of refinement, beauty and culture could help but be enthralled at the sensitivity of Mozart's musical compositions, a sensitivity characteristic of the ruling 11. Sensitivity is the soulmate of compassion, and we know that Mozart's life was directed in this vein. His dedication to work precipitated an untimely end, for it so depleted his health that he died at the age of thirty-five. He left no money, for he barely earned sufficient to feed himself and his family. This is not uncommon among those ruling 11 people who have discovered a vital essence to their lives; for money, to them, is never an end in itself.

Personal hardship is apparent when there is a heavy incidence of 7s in such people's numbers. Mozart had two 7s on his Birthchart (as did Beethoven — in fact, they had rather similar Birthcharts). These 7s imply the depth of personal sacrifice each had to endure in order to achieve his life's ambitions. History confirms these assessments. Sacrifices occur invariably in the areas of health, love and/or money, the intention of such great masters being to develop a level of higher understanding which is to be shared with those who are ready.

RULING NUMBER 22/4

This is the master number. People born with the Ruling Number

22/4 possess unlimited potential and often make their mark in life by achieving seemingly impossible goals. But there are two distinct types of ruling 22/4 — the aware and the unaware. The difference between them is extreme. The former benefit from the successful mastery of any aspect of life into which they are directed; the latter drift into a lazy indifference and become almost useless misfits. The number 22 occupies a special place in symbolic philosophy. It represents the circle which encompasses all, the nothing and yet the everything, the infinite. In the science of numbers, 22 represents a doubling of the highest spiritual power, (double 11), complemented by the intense practicality of the 4 — a unique combination of the utmost benefit in earthly life. Because of its special combination of spiritual and physical powers, this Ruling Number is always written as 22/4 and verbally expressed as twenty-two four. Of all the Ruling Numbers, 22/4 is the most seldom found. Only one total of birthdate numbers can result in 22, and the exceedingly high responsibilities this brings with it are such as to attract only the most evolved souls seeking reincarnation. Experience indicates that only around one percent of the population possess this Ruling Number.

Purpose   As human life continues to evolve through stages of progressive enlightenment there will always be people of outstanding leadership whose purpose is to guide such evolution. This they achieve in much the same way as some outstanding directors guide the unfolding of a movie or a play — they might take a minor role in it themselves, but never the starring role, preferring to guide from behind the scenes where the decisions are made and the entire all-over design is formulated. In whatever walk of life they find themselves, if 22/4s are living positively, they are invariably at the core of the organisation. With the approach of the new age the role of these people is particularly crucial, for their personal enlightenment is a beacon whose light will illumine the Path and guide countless others, many of whom will not realise from whence came the guidance and encouragement. It is generally not characteristic of ruling 22/4s to be found in the limelight of human affairs; in fact, they work far better in partial anonymity, so long as they gain sufficient recognition by way of respect and co-operation to facilitate their work.

Best Expression   To achieve any semblance of their potential, ruling 22/4s need a first-rate education. Many of them spend a great deal of their time in studies, always seeking to better themselves. They realise that by this means they are better equipped to help others. These are people who must be allowed to work without constrictions, for they become most frustrated if they work under direction for too long. The rate at which these people learn is quite surprising, as though they have done most things in previous lives and are merely reacquainting themselves with the current modes of expression. Little wonder they constantly rise to leadership in whatever they do.

Distinctive Traits

One of the most noticeable traits of ruling 22/4s is their apparent lack of emotion. They regard complete emotional control as being fundamental to their purpose. So it is for this reason that they adopt it, rather than from any desire to be exclusive or difficult to understand. Actually they are very sensitive people, with deeply loving natures, although only their closer friends come to realise this. Ruling 22/4 people rarely fail to accept a challenge, especially if it involves human welfare. They will be found in some of the most difficult and seemingly dangerous environments, but are usually cool and careful in the execution of whatever work they are directing. Their capacity for responsibility is limitless and, because of this, others come to depend on them, too much perhaps, producing both an unfair burden on the 22/4 and encouraging a little laziness on the part of the other person.

Negative Tendencies to be Surmounted

Most 22/4 people readily recognise many of their strengths and capably employ them. The few who do not, or who are drawn into a materialistic environment, take on all the negative aspects of the ruling 4, but worse. They become little better than misfits, with an obsession for money, in the quest for which they will brook little interference. They become unhappy, aloof and insensitive to refinement. This often creates deep loneliness and excessive self-centredness in such people, whether they are found at the head of a large organisation or doing manual work under direction. Rehabilitation from these depths demands great patience, understanding and unstinting loving tenderness. As all ruling 22/4 people are fond of art, rhythm, dancing and most forms of music, the use of these avenues of expression will be found of great help in bringing about balanced emotions and a more positive attitude.

Recommended Development

For all ruling 22/4s it is important to ensure that life provides a balance of work and pleasure. To be sure, they have such a considerable aptitude for work that they often dismiss pleasures as a waste of time. Their development along artistic and cultural lines through hobbies — such as singing, dancing, painting, writing or similar pursuits — will greatly help them to express their feelings more capably, and loosen up emotionally. They must always endeavour to have good academic training and are never too old to get it. (Lack of opportunity in childhood is never a valid excuse.)

Most Suitable Vocations

These people are suited to work as leaders in business and cultural organisations; artists; teachers or reformers; writers; diplomats; efficiency experts; administrators.

Capsule Summary

This is the master number; whose bearers have the most extreme levels of personal responsibility; they are highly intuitive, with a very tight rein on their emotions and an intense concern for human welfare.

Personality Example

Margaret Thatcher, born October 13, 1925.

The choice of Margaret Thatcher for this example was made for a very important reason: she is a very powerful person who has assumed control of an ailing country. She is probably the only person who has the ability to steer Britain back to a sound economy — as though she were the 'last chance.' May she be only one of many women who have the courage of their convictions to enter the field of government and correct the inhumanities that so many thoughtless men have perpetrated upon this beautiful planet.

Margaret Thatcher typifies a ruling 22/4. She is charming, highly intuitive and, in fact, possesses all the virtues in the above capsule summary. And she will need them in her onerous task. Indeed, she has to believe herself to possess almost limitless strength and managerial ability to achieve any measure of success in restoring Great Britain to a position of world leadership. Her sense of fair play will be guided by her acute intuitiveness so that she will not be hoodwinked into leading her country further along the road of useless compromise to placate the selfish demands of those warring factions which have hitherto fuelled the conflict. She is a person of resolve who will get her way to the ultimate benefit of all the people.

Strong determination is reinforced by the arrow 1-5-9 on Margaret Thatcher's Birthchart. This is intensified by the Arrow of the Planner (described in Stage 7), so she has a unique power base upon which to develop her plans for Britain's recovery. Her Day Number 4 and her balanced Mental Plane (the 3 and 9 on the Birthchart) are further aids in this direction.

In summary, this is a unique person. No world leader is better equipped to undertake such a momentous task than Margaret Thatcher. Undoubtedly, she will prove to the world that the talents of women in government should not be so shamefully overlooked. For what the world needs now, more than ever, is compassion, intuitive guidance and leadership by selfless example. In short, every country needs a Margaret Thatcher.

STAGE 5
The Birthchart—Your Formula

The medium through which the essential characteristics of a person are obtained is the date of birth written in terms of its component numbers. Individual numbers of the birthdate are then placed on a simple chart for analysis. This we call the Birthchart, for it portrays from birth the pattern of basic strengths and weaknesses — the inherent formula, so to speak, of the person's individuality. Choose a few birthdates and practise the following method:

Step 1   The birthdate must first be written in its full numerical terms. January is 1, going through to December, which is 12. Thus, July 25, 1968 is written 7-25-1968.

Step 2   The Birthchart is now constructed of four lines — two horizontal parallel lines intersected by two vertical lines, similarly spaced, to form nine spaces of equal size. The Birthchart is always drawn in the same way, thus:

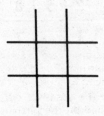

Step 3   We must now place the numbers of the birthdate on the Birthchart. (When empty, the chart represents a person not yet born — its nine spaces as yet have no numbers.) Each number always occupies the same space, no matter how often it occurs in the birthdate or how many other numbers are missing from the birthdate. The full Birthchart, if one of every number were present, would appear thus:

3	6	9
2	5	8
1	4	7

This chart represents a perfect person, one who has complete balance. Of course, this can never be, any more than it is possible for one birthdate to provide these numbers in this or any other era. In practice, a Birthchart will always have some empty spaces — at least two, and up to seven spaces can be empty. Inevitably, there will be some duplication of numbers as well, although a very small percentage of birthdates will be found to have no duplication. For example, a person born on July 25, 1968 would have his birthdate represented thus:

7-25-1968

This would result in the following Birthchart, seen to have seven spaces occupied and no duplication of numbers:

	6	9
2	5	8
1		7

At the other end of the scale we occasionally find a birthdate with only two spaces filled on the Birthchart. This will be found to contain a heavy concentration of at least one particular number. An example is a person born November 10, 1911. The birthdate is set forth thus:

11-10-1911

Now we see a very different Birthchart to the previous example:

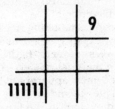

Please note that the zero is omitted when setting up the Birthchart, as it has no value in this phase of numerological analysis. Its presence does, however, reduce the number of numbers appearing in the birthdate and on the Birthchart. To this extent we can see that zero sometimes implies certain modifications; at other times its presence can help avoid too much concentration of numbers on the Birthchart. In practice, the zero will be found to provide a valuable balancing factor in the personality.

Step 4   With the Birthchart complete we are now ready to analyse its general meaning, to discover the plane upon which the person basically expresses most fluently. This should precede the analysis of the component numbers of the Birthchart. If the Birthchart is well balanced such expression might expand over two planes, or even over all three. To comprehend the three basic planes of expression let us again refer to the full Birthchart and observe the positions of these planes:

3	6	9	Mental Plane (thinking, intellect)
2	5	8	Spiritual Plane (feeling, emotion)
1	4	7	Practical Plane (doing)

Each of the three horizontal sets of spaces forms a separate plane of expression. If a person's Birthchart has an equal distribution of numbers over the three planes his basic expression should be similarly balanced. If a particular concentration of numbers on any one or two of the planes is apparent, we can recognise the general nature of the person's inherent expression and motivation from the characteristics of the plane(s).

Mental Plane   The numbers on the top line of the Birthchart indicate emphasis in the direction of the mind and mental processes, including thinking, analysing, imagining, creating, etc. They are the numbers of conscious awareness, when used in combination with the positive spiritual powers; of facts, figures and prejudices when used in combination with material powers. The difference between the two applications becomes apparent when we recognise the distinction between intelligence and intellect — the first manifesting in the former, the second evident in the latter application.

Definitions, by their very nature, tend to limit. Therefore, we shall not attempt to define intelligence but rather to explain it as being the wise use of universal knowledge, applied with awareness and understanding. Intellect is more easily defined because it is more limited, being the accumulated memory bank of worldly notions gathered by the experiences of the senses and by parental and academic training. The intellect can certainly aid in the development of the intelligence if it is directed toward improving the quality of life. When employed negatively the intellect can be an encumbrance to the intelligence, thwarting its development by befogging the issues and leading to incorrect and shallow conclusions.

Spiritual Plane   The centre line of the Birthchart represents the realms of feeling through which the mental is related to the practical. It is called the Spiritual Plane because if embraces qualities of a spiritual or metaphysical (beyond the physical) nature such as intuition, feelings and emotions. At this point, it is helpful to understand the meaning of emotion. Emotions are really reactive expressions of somewhat uncontrolled feelings. Literally, the word emotion means backward motion. Thus, for the duration of their expression, emotions imply reactions to circumstances outside us which, for that time, overwhelm us because we have let them gain control. For that period we have lost self-mastery, our individuality being submerged by the external factors to which we are reacting. These reactions need not be detrimental so long as they provide purpose or pleasure. The most appropriate use of emotions is to lend variety to the scale of human expression.

Practical Plane   The nature of man's physical expression is generally revealed by numbers on this plane. These numbers — 1, 4 and 7 — are his 'doing' numbers. When employed positively they facilitate tangible expression by word and action, efficient organising, instruction and practical involvement. Negatively expressed, they indicate egotism, self-aggrandisement, materialism and, inevitably, sacrifice.

STAGE 6
Meanings of the Individual Numbers on the Birthchart

THE NUMBER 1 ON THE CHART

Located at the beginning of the Practical Plane, the number 1 refers to the expression of the physical body in terms of its relationship to the outside world. It is usually a very good indication of the extent to which a person reacts to other people and circumstances (the immediate environment). This denotes to the thinking person the degree of his self-control — or its lack. As the key to self-expression, this number is the foundation of the personality.

One 1   Birthdates with a single 1 belong to people who have some difficulty in self-expression. This does not mean that they cannot speak well, but rather the difficulty lies in their inability to give clear explanations of their real selves, their inner feelings.

Although they are often good orators, an argument concerning their own feelings causes them to fare badly, as they fall short of being able to put into words their attitudes or conduct. Until they develop adequate self-mastery — a product of maturity and understanding — self-expression will not come easily to them.

They will sometimes say the wrong thing intentionally, to hurt or to offend or to create an early defence, whether or not the need is present. They must learn to think before speaking — the spoken word is hard to retract and hurt feelings are so difficult to mend.

Two 1s   These people have the gift of self-expression. This is a most valuable possession and one which should be used wisely. Care should be taken to avoid intolerance of those who are not so blessed.

These people have a balanced outlook which enables them to see both sides of a situation or proposal. They can support either with equal enthusiasm, giving them an extremely broad understanding.

Three 1s   There are two distinctly different types of people here.

Chatterboxes are the people with three 1s most frequently met —

45

always bright and interesting people who involve themselves in many activities and generally find life to be most enjoyable, seeking to share that enjoyment with others.

The quiet people with three 1s will generally be found to have no numbers on the Spiritual Plane (the Arrow of Hypersensitivity), making them introspective and somewhat shy. Their natural tendency to be bright and breezy is inhibited by this sensitivity, except when with their closest friends. These people will find their best expression in writing, where their thoughts flow more freely, unhampered by other people or situations.

Four 1s
These are quiet and sensitive people. Due to their acute inability to verbally express themselves as they would like, they are easily misunderstood. This brings much pain to their highly sensitive natures, but they quickly learn to hide this with a smile, although inwardly their emotions cause them to suffer.

They have deep feeling for others, but do not voice such thoughts easily, due to their emotional constraints. It is important for their own happiness that they attain emotional control by realising that emotions are basically the reactions of a misunderstanding sensitivity. As they learn to know their Inner Selves they will feel less inhibited and become freer to express, rather than suppress, their inner feelings and their appreciation of life and of people.

Five and More 1s
With five, six or seven 1s on the Birthchart, an increasingly heavy imbalance is created to compound the difficulty of vocal self-expression. Their young lives can indeed be quite sad, due to being so misunderstood, often creating an aloofness, an inner loneliness. This tends to make them overly attentive to their personal selves, making them obsessive about their appearances and actions. Such egoism can lead to mental unbalance. It must be especially guarded against by those in charge of young children who have this heavy concentration of 1s. It is vitally important for all these people to elevate their consciousness by becoming involved in communicating through writing or one of the other expressive arts such as painting, music and pottery. (It is interesting to note that the occurrence of seven 1s in a birthdate is extremely rare, fortunately, appearing only once a century. It last occurred on November 11, 1911 — the last occasion for 200 years.)

Some Personality Examples
It is important to note that the number of 1s present on their Birthcharts bears no relationship to the degree of success achieved by people during their lifetimes. Of the twenty-five famous people chosen to illustrate this book, a rather even sprinkling of varying numbers of 1s appears on the Birthcharts; up to five 1s. Each has

something of importance to convey about the self-expression of the bearer.

A classic example of one 1 is shown on the Birthchart of Senator Edward Kennedy. From this, we learn that a person can hold a very important place in his country's government, even to the extent of being recognised as a powerful orator, yet possess an inherent difficulty in expressing his innermost feelings to those with whom he is most intimate. On such occasions, he finds that his words do not flow so freely, especially when called upon to justify or explain a personal desire or action. This often creates misunderstandings, for his defensiveness will be expressed in an evasive or aggressive manner, unintentionally offending others.

The effectiveness of two 1s in providing a well-balanced self-expression can be recognised in the vocal and literary outputs of Germaine Greer. In her role as a reforming feminist, she has accepted constant exposure to demands to justify this intensely personal mission. Her mastery of interviews and the fluent expression of her cause have brought her world-wide recognition.

Many famous people possess three 1s on their Birthcharts; in fact forty percent of the personality examples chosen to illustrate this book have three 1s. They tend to be more ego-motivated people than those with one or two 1s, and are generally bright, interesting people with an engaging public image. This helps to make them excellent media personalities, as is exemplified by Caroline Jones. Compare her friendly mode of interviewing with the more abrasive style of Michael Willesee and you have an illustration of the difference often encountered between three 1s (Jones) and one 1 (Willesee) in similar roles. Each is an excellent interviewer, but on different levels of communication — the former is encouraging; the latter is challenging, especially when his inner feelings are involved.

When Birthcharts reveal five 1s or more, we should seek the best means whereby guidance can be directed to help these people maintain balance in their outlooks. Discover in which direction their aloofness tends to manifest itself and you tap into their egocentricity and can assist them in recognising the source of their loneliness. In the case of Joh Bjelke-Petersen, his emotions tend to make him aloof because he finds great difficulty in expressing them in a controlled manner which will bring pleasure to all parties involved. Thus he often constricts his emotions until they burst out in an unpleasant, egocentric way. His best avenue for gaining control of this vital aspect of expression is to commune more with nature, by hiking, gardening, etc., especially with a helpful and harmonious companion. In this manner, the exceptional strength of the five 1s will be directed towards balancing the unprotected Spiritual Plane and its acute sensitivity.

THE NUMBER 2 ON THE CHART

Located as the first number on the Spiritual Plane, 2 is the key to sensitivity, intuition and feeling. After 1 and 9, 2 is the most common number found in birthdates, appearing in fifty to sixty percent of those encountered in this millenium. A 2 can be quite a blessing because it provides us with a reliable guide to the degree of our sensitivity and our intuition. As these faculties develop we acquire an improved understanding of ourselves, of people, of life and of all creation.

In the next millenium (the years 2000 to 2999), no birthdate will be without a 2, an indication of how much more sensitivity and intuition will then prevail in human affairs. No 2 in the birthdate does not imply total absence of these traits, but rather the need of a greater personal effort to develop them to the point of reliable guidance — so helpful in human relationships.

One 2   Birthdates with a single 2 indicate an increased degree of sensitivity and intuition, but sometimes not enough for adequate protection of individuality in the highly competitive, somewhat artificial social and commercial world of today. It is not uncommon for these people to have their feelings hurt, but they do have a basis for building self-control and can learn to be less reactive.

They need guidance onto the path of best expression for their nature in a direction which will easily be found from their Ruling Number. Life will be easier for them if they try to avoid the rat race and learn to be themselves without the intensity of competition.

Two 2s   These people are blessed with the prospect of balanced sensitivity and intuition — so long as they are prepared to apply these gifts. (Any virtue not used invariably deteriorates).

Their innate perception places them among the most intuitive of all people. This generally gives rise to a high intelligence, based on an acute ability for understanding people and circumstances. They have a very reliable guide in their first impressions by which almost instant and accurate opinions of people and concepts are made. Sincerity or insincerity in others is thereby easily detected.

Such balanced abilities tend to draw these people into becoming very involved in human affairs.

Three 2s   Here we find an imbalance leading to hypersensitivity. This can become quite a load to carry if not properly understood.

Spending so much of their time in a world of their own feelings, these people can become quite aloof. They are inclined to suffer deeply because they are easily hurt and cannot always understand or express the feelings thus created. This can cause them to become quite reactive, unless they have learned to master their emotions. Otherwise, they can impulsively say hurtful things or make fun of people without actually meaning to be harmful. Such are their attempts to defend their feelings and allay their fears of being hurt.

As children, these people often become great imitators in an attempt to hide their keen sensitivity and avoid having their feelings hurt. Parents should be especially careful to recognise this situation and help these children to attain control of their emotions by developing self-confidence. This is best achieved along the Path indicated by their Ruling Number.

Four 2s   This exceptionally high level of impressionability has to be carefully and continuously disciplined or it will easily erupt into severe misrepresentations which are invariably accompanied by bad temper, sarcasm and spite.

These people are often extremely impatient, with an unreliable intuition which acts to confuse and mislead them into placing confidence in the wrong people. They have a tendency to spontaneous over-reaction which can make them quite volatile and, if not checked, lead to unbalance.

Extreme patience and understanding must be shown by friends (of which they often have very few) and especially by immediate family. Although these people comprise only a fraction of one percent of the population they feature in a much higher proportion of marital breakups, homes for the needy and refuges for the disturbed and homeless. Their lives are often very lonely, but this can be avoided if they open themselves to wise counselling and guidance by one who is trained to recognise the nature of the imbalance and its purpose — to learn to firmly apply self-control in the emotional arena, to relax and flow with life, rather than be at variance with it.

Five 2s   An extremely rare occurrence, with a frequency of only twice a century. It last occurred on December 22, 1922 and this writer has met only one person with such a birthdate. (The contact was in the course of business, but it was clear that this person was hiding a deep heartache and avoided any conversation which so much as alluded to his personal self.) Such individuals are potentially likely suicides, with lives of bitter disappointments, frustrations and disillusionments. They need extremely concentrated and devoted guidance, for they will try others' patience to the extreme.

Some Personality Examples   As the number of sensitivity and intuition, it is not surprising that 2 is found on the

49

Birthcharts of many famous people, especially those associated with the arts and culture. This is not to say that people without a 2 are never found among such luminaries, but rather that those with a 2 have the distinct natural advantage of heightened awareness potential. But many people without a 2 learn to develop such awareness — an important achievement. Women invariably succeed best at this for by nature they are more intuitive.

Caroline Jones affords a timely example of how a woman can capably develop her intuition and sensitivity, yet possess no 2 on her Birthchart. Rupert Murdoch, on the other hand, has not been so successful in this regard, although he relies on his two 3s, for they provide him with a sagacious cunning by means of which he achieves results far different from those people often predict of his methods (especially apparent in his corporate raiding).

Michael Willesee, Bob Hawke and Don Dunstan all possess two 2s and all have this balanced intuitiveness counter-weighted by the Arrow of Scepticism (see page 70). This does not detract from their deep-rooted sensitivity other than in their expression of it — it causes them to investigate and assess things prior to acceptance. This makes Willesee such a perceptive interviewer, Hawke an excellent negotiator and Dunstan so successful with his audiences — whether from the political stage or the entertainment one.

As the manuscript for this book was being completed Senator Edward Kennedy announced his long-awaited intention of running for the 1980 U.S.A. presidential nomination. He has a very strong chance of being ultimately elected fortieth President of the United States and would commence office with a flourish of creative activity, but it would be shortlived — indeed, this author cannot see him in office for more than a year, for his life comes to a crisis in 1981 (probably in July). (His Personal Year 7, under these circumstances, implies a special danger to his life.) In spite of his seeming national popularity, Teddy Kennedy has made some avowed enemies. Most probably his four 2s have caused this, for he has not used this tremendous power of intuition wisely. When combined with the lack of a 4 (impatience), the one 1 on the Birthchart and the aspect of overt criticism of the ruling 3 used negatively, this force can be seen to manifest itself in such extremes of bad temper, biting sarcasm and spite that forgiveness by those so offended is out of the question. He does not use his intuition wisely, often placing confidence in those who least justify it. These factors will lead to his downfall unless rapidly recognised and checked.

THE NUMBER 3 ON THE CHART

Not only is this the first number on the Mental Plane, the 3 is also the most powerful of the mind numbers. Whereas with 1s and 2s the most ideal balance and power were found to be when either was represented on the Birthchart as a pair, with the 3 and higher numbers on the chart right up to 9, the single number generally implies the most balanced strength. The concentrated power of these higher vibrations when compounded invariably creates an imbalance, demanding extreme self-discipline to a degree to which few people will apply themselves. The absence of a 3 from a Birthchart does not necessarily imply mental weakness. Rather, it indicates that the person needs to exert greater effort in the mental spheres, especially if their Ruling Number is not a mind number (Stage 4), or their Sun Sign is not a Head Sign (Stage 11). There is often a tendency towards mental laziness when a 3 is absent from the chart.

One 3   These people have the blessing of higher thought analysis, mental deductive powers and retentive memory, especially when balanced with one 9 on the chart. The power of the single 3 is such as to strengthen these attributes, and encourage their most balanced expression.

As mental strength is a vital foundation for the cultivation of a balanced, optimistic understanding of life, these people generally have happy dispositions and can readily apply themselves to most tasks with the prospect of success.

Two 3s   With this increased mental alertness comes a strengthening of the imagination and intensification of literary ability. Such power has to be carefully disciplined to facilitate its most useful and most balanced expression. This potentially high level of mental expression could otherwise lead to such imbalances as antisocial behaviour or a persecution complex (imagination allowed to go uncontrolled). To facilitate self-discipline, the practice of meditation is a very valuable exercise, together with memory training, the comprehension of moderation and the development of the intuition. This will enable wisdom to guide these people's thought processes for the benefit of all concerned. Otherwise, their highly active brains will place too much significance on imagination, to the detriment of objective planning, investigation and deduction. In so doing, they tend to lose track of reality.

Three 3s   With even greater emphasis on mental activities and expression, these people often lose contact with reality, inducing an isolation which brings loneliness into their lives. Their fertile imaginations are so intent on thinking ahead and planning that they find difficulty in relating to other people. Consequently, these

51

people rarely develop close friendships. They are sometimes so absorbed in their own mental adventures that they become quite oblivious to people speaking to them or to things about them. This can be infuriating to others and potentially dangerous to themselves should they be in a hazardous situation.

Such unbalanced concentration does not equip these people to see things in true perspective. Their introversion makes them distrustful of other people and often quite argumentative. The best way to help these people is to encourage them to give their attention to the world around them through the increased use of their hearts and hands, thereby expressing their imaginations in a practical, considerate way. This vital form of help demands great patience and understanding from the helper.

Four 3s   This unusual combination can only occur on five days during one month in a century — it last occurred on March 31, 1933.

Excessive imagination and mental hyperactivity of these people can bring them to the point of intense fear, worry and confusion.

They do not care for physical concerns and are generally quite impractical in outlook — a very serious weakness.

As understanding them demands so much of others, they rarely have close friends. Yet these people have the utmost need for the help of a patient and wise person who can guide them in directing their emphasis away from their intense mentality. This will help them to become more balanced individuals. These people are often plagued with phobias and obsessions when allowed to dwell too much within themselves. They must be encouraged to make more use of their hands in pragmatic expression, such as in dressmaking, hairdressing, landscaping, interior decorating, etc.

THE NUMBER 4 ON THE CHART

Symbolically, the 4 represents containment and regularity, as depicted by the square. It is a practical and material number, located squarely in the centre of the Practical Plane. People with this number on their Birthchart are generally tidy and meticulous. Birthcharts without a 4 indicate a degree of impatience in those people, but this is easily overcome by conscious attention to detail and to other people's needs.

One 4   These individuals have a natural identity with the practical. This can be capably expressed over a wide range of activities, including organisational, technical, financial and/or physical activities (such as gardening, manual arts and building). The particular avenue of expression will be indicated by their Ruling Number.

Preferring to work with concrete rather than theoretical concepts, these people are often sceptical of obscurities. They prefer practice to principle.

Too much emphasis on the physical can make them somewhat materialistic, allowing a hardness to develop in their personality. They must use their natural patience to avoid an unbalanced materialism by nurturing concern and compassion for others in their daily contacts. Only in this manner will they attain lasting friendships and happiness.

Two 4s   Greater weight in this material direction can lead to an unbalanced outlook which relates everything to the physical.

The strong utilitarian abilities of these people must be trained for capable expression by balancing a sound mental concept with appreciation for things aesthetic.

If their Ruling Number is spiritual or mental these people will find greater assistance in rising above the physical than if the Ruling Number is also physical (a 4, 7 or 10). A well-chosen name will also be of help (Stage 12).

The more 4s in the birthdate, the greater care must be exercised in choosing friends. These people will benefit from the company of others who enjoy the beauties and cultural qualities in life, thereby developing better balance in outlook and diminishing harshness in themselves. Especially should they endeavour to steer clear of the hard-drinking, heavy-smoking style of person.

Three 4s   Even greater difficulty is experienced by these people in rising above materialistic and physical involvements. Those who recognise this need must employ great effort and will need diligent guidance.

Many people with this aspect feel the pull towards hard, manual work and persist with it, not realising that their lesson is to master it, then to rise above it to acquire necessary balance through mental and spiritual expression. They must guard against relating everything to the hard and callous physical, and going overboard about such concerns as neatness. It is important to be neat and tidy, but not to make a fetish of it and allow it to assume the dimensions of an obsession.

These people have a tendency to weakness in their lower limbs, generally about the knees. Special care should be taken in work and, particularly, at play to avoid exposing knees, legs and feet to unnecessary hazard.

Four 4s   This is another extremely rare occurrence, happening only three times a century — on the 4th, 14th and 24th of April during the forty-fifth year of each century. It last occurred on April 24, 1944.

Due to the extreme weight of the physical thus created, very special care must be exercised in the activities of these individuals. There is a critical weakness in the lower limbs and, of the few people with this number grouping, most are, for some period of their life, crippled.

Extreme patience is demanded with these people as they are highly sceptical of non-physical (metaphysical) concepts, taking notice only of cold, hard facts. Never tell them about numerology or the occult, as both are beyond their ability to comprehend.

Some Personality Examples   In practice, we find that around twenty-five percent of all birthdates have at least one 4 in them. Yet in our twenty-five examples of famous people, only two have a 4 on their Birthchart. This is not to imply that one needs be devoid of a 4 to become famous in life, but it does reveal to us that the impatience indicated by the lack of 4 on the Birthchart can become a very real driving force in the attainment of one's goals. To be motivated by impatience will result in a drain on nervous energy. These people must ensure they do not become enervated: they should take sufficient time to relax during the course of each day. The consequence of omission will be chronic illness in later life, a time when their years of earlier effort should be rewarded.

The two examples of 4 on the Birthchart are Ita Buttrose and Michael Willesee. (Interestingly, another of the media personalities chosen, Kerry Packer, is a ruling 4.) Both people are known to prefer concrete concepts, as opposed to hypothetical ones, both are very practical and extremely capable organisers and both give the occasional appearance that a certain hardness is creeping into their manner — a tendency with this number which has to be guarded against.

THE NUMBER 5 ON THE CHART

The special position of this number in the centre of the chart created an important need for its understanding, for it governs the intensity of human feelings. As the second number on the Spiritual (feeling) Plane, 5 exerts a strong influence on the intensity of the feelings and the strength of will required to translate them into action.

One 5   This helps to create a balanced emotional control by which the sensitivities develop as reliable instinctive guides in choosing suitable courses of action, rather than responding to situations by thoughtless reactions.

In providing a valuable protection to their sensitivities, one 5 strengthens the disciplines of fortitude and compassion noticeably, creating what many people regard as strength of character.

In understanding their own feelings these people, (especially if they also have two 2s on their Birthchart) develop a deep appreciation for the feelings of others.

Two 5s
These individuals are frequently recognised by their driving inner intensity, expressed in their powerful staring eyes and furrowed brows. Intensified determination gives them an air of great confidence and self-assurance which is often more wishful than factual. As they grow into maturity, this self-assurance tends to diminish to mere bravado as if they find it difficult to cope with emotional, domestic and/or vocational troubles.

To the annoyance and exasperation of those with whom these people are closely associated, the drive and enthusiasm stimulated by their two 5s can become overbearing. This provokes misunderstandings and some troublesome situations in their home and work environments. So intense will their attitudes become that a state of deep emotional turmoil often develops, creating ulcers and associated health problems in the region of the solar plexus.

Special care must be taken by these people to exercise emotional control, or they could easily become dependent on drugs or sexuality for the release of their pent-up emotional energy. Particularly during the period preceding mealtimes, they must make certain that their emotions do not take charge or they will suffer from acute indigestion. A cup of naturally soothing herbal tea, such as chamomile, taken about half an hour before the meal, and some soft relaxing music with the meal, will be greatly beneficial to them.

Three 5s
Such power as this is too difficult for most people to effectively handle. Fortunately, few are born with this extreme intensity of drive and feeling.

Very special and careful training in self-discipline has to be a part of the early lives of these people, placing unique responsibilities upon the parents (who, rarely equipped for such a task, often throw up their hands in despair through failure to understand this type of child).

Such a heavy abundance of power must be used constructively or it will become an egocentric barrier to social happiness by making other people look painfully insignificant. Extreme care must be taken to think well before speaking or acting, especially where there is any risk to people's sensitivities.

Four 5s
The rarity of this combination (occurring only three times a century, the last being on May 25, 1955) is fortunate as it indicates a life of great risk and overwhelming intensity of feeling.

Severe accidents often beset these people, the purpose being to slow them down and force them to think deeply and carefully, so that they react less and act with more care.

They find life very difficult to understand without extremely sensitive and patient, yet firm, guidance.

Some Personality Examples

Although it occurs no more frequently in birthdates than does the 4, the 5 is found in six of the twenty-five birthdates of famous people chosen for this book. This is not surprising when we recognise that the 5 is a powerful aid to the development of the will and to aspiring towards personal freedom.

The personal intensity created by the double 5 in the centre of the Birthchart should always attract the immediate interest of the numerologist. This is exemplified in the birthdate of Xavier Herbert. It will be found that the double 5 often inspires enough personal forcefulness to create friction in personal dealings with others, especially on matters concerning individual freedom.

His compassionate and tireless work for the Australian Aboriginal cause illustrates and utilises the potential indicated by Xavier Herbert's Birthchart. This is complemented by his prodigious literary output, for he is recognised as one of Australia's leading authors of today.

Of further special interest in his Birthchart is the presence of only a single arrow (of determination) and the fact that all his numbers are to be found only along this arrow. Determination, pivoting around a double 5, is under the control of spiritual sensitivity and is related closely to the solar plexus. With his birthdate numbers revealing him to be a ruling 22/4, Xavier Herbert (born May 15, 1901) is a man possessed of a powerful mission.

The emotional intensity of the double 5, under the powerful control of the ruling 22/4, indicates how easily Xavier Herbert will either suppress his feelings or will spontaneously react if he thinks the situation is under his control. To many, he will thus appear unpredictable and mysterious. For others, this apparent capriciousness stimulates interest and even fascination, for it gives rise to a lively personality. However, care must be taken that such oscillation of moods does not lead to nerve-induced illness. Hypertension, strokes, heart attacks and the like are not uncommon consequences of suppressed or ragged emotions. One must learn that emotions are intended to be used, not to use us in uncontrolled reactiveness.

THE NUMBER 6 ON THE CHART

Located in the centre of the Mental Plane, the 6 occupies a unique position of mental power which can be as constructive, when used positively, as it is destructive, when used negatively. Its primary control is over the power of creativity, by which the five senses are brought into a fertile union with mind power.

One 6   This potent number of creativity finds its most common expression in a deep love of the home. However, its higher expression is found in artistic creation of a more personal nature, such as in pottery, painting and similar disciplines where all senses harmonise to form beauty.

These people generally have a very close tie to either their own home or the home of someone dear to them. They revel in domestic responsibilities, creating with ease the atmosphere of harmony and love in the home.

As they grow in awareness, they are readily able to elevate and expand their creative powers toward broader fields of social expression, such as in art and human welfare.

Two 6s   Doubling of this creative power can easily cause an unsetting in people who have not learned to understand and discipline themselves.

Worry and overanxiety about the home and loved ones is made more intense for these by the double 6, inducing adverse reactions upon the nervous system. Their interests must be directed beyond the limitations of the home so that their attention is taken away from that which devitalises them. Their vocation must be a creative one which permits them full expression. In that work they greatly need to be inspired with confidence by understanding direction. They must be guided, never pushed or threatened. Love and appreciation are vital to them, acting as balm to their nervous system.

These people require much more rest than most. They must learn to meditate before going to bed to ensure that their sleep is deeply restful. When possible, they should take a siesta during the afternoon.

Some important dietary guidance, which is of general help to people today, is especially beneficial to those who are inclined towards worry and anxiety. Their foods should always be fresh and free from chemicals used for preservation, flavouring or colouring. Artificial chemicals added to foods often cause severe irritation to the nervous system, as proven in research on hyperactive children by Dr Ben Feingold and others in the field. One cannot go wrong with a diet based on fresh fruits and vegetables, primarily vegetarian, for modern meats contain far too many chemicals to be considered natural foods.

Three 6s With the multiplying of 6s on the Birthchart come increasing home worries, often causing situations of utter domestic confusion.

Acute overprotectiveness of their children and the fear of their growing up and departing from the home usually cause these individuals to become extremely possessive parents. This can only be avoided by directing the attention away from the home at every opportunity. Art or music are especially suited to help in achieving a necessary diversion.

Their intense powers of creativity are usually too difficult for one mere mortal to handle, hence the vital need for devoted understanding from the spouse.

Special care must be taken to avert the occurrence of a nervous breakdown which, for most people in this group, is a warning from the body that it cannot take any further emotional turmoil. Again, special attention to rest and diet will be of invaluable assistance.

Four 6s This accumulation of 6s occurs only three times a century, on June 6, 16 and 26. In this century the year was 1966.

It indicates quite exceptional creativity but, human nature being as unthinkingly emotional as it is, such power cannot be properly expressed until these people are well into the mature years of life; and only then if a spartan self-discipline has been practised during the earlier years.

For the most part, this combination indicates severe emotional problems which often lead to a neurotic incapacity to handle life, demanding very special counselling and extreme tolerance from others.

THE NUMBER 7 ON THE CHART

As the last number on the Practical Plane, 7 represents a special function of human life. It indicates the amount of learning one must amass by that form of personal experience known as sacrifice. However, its broader, more metaphysical meaning implies a detachment from possessions as being necessary for the unfolding of the soul.

One 7 As part of the vital learning process, sacrifices in matters of love or money or health will be encountered when this number appears on the Birthchart.

Those whose charts contain one 7 are obliged to adopt the precept that from every experience in which some loss is sustained a most important lesson will emerge to assist them on the endless Path towards perfection, the course of the soul's unfolding. Of course, man is rarely aware of the ultimate purpose for which all his lessons are intended; consequently, these sacrifices are often bemoaned when only their materialistic implications are considered. It is therefore important to gain every measure of understanding from each lesson, thereby avoiding its repetition and further losses.

Development of such understanding of life generally brings with it an increasing interest in the occult, the study of metaphysical truths which are so often erroneously regarded as mysteries.

Two 7s   The compounding of this number implies the increased intensity of the lessons to be undergone, and often generates in these people a deep philosophical understanding of life and keen interest in the occult.

Sacrifices are usually experienced in two of the three categories of love, money and health to underline the value of the lesson concerned. These heavier losses bring with them greater unfoldment, preparing these people for taking on enlightened powers for healing, guidance and compassion.

When not living positively, these people fail to develop that indispensable philosophical understanding; instead, they lament their losses, accuse life of being unfair and become grumpy, complaining individuals.

Three 7s   Superficially, this weighty accumulation of 7s appears to result in particularly sad lives brought about by losses in love, money and health.

Such losses test these people's powers of fortitude and enormous strength can be gained from these experiences. This can make for the emergence of truly remarkable people, valuable friends whose outlook on life grows with maturity, achieving almost infinite depths of wisdom.

There are others to be found in this group and they (unfortunately, the ones more commonly encountered in this affluent society) can develop into manic depressives or become so dejected as to be encumbrances to family, friends and society. They are extremely negative and feel life to be a huge burden. To them, the sun is always obscured by a heavy cloud.

Four 7s   Lecturing in Toronto, Ontario, during the month of July, 1977, I was feeling deep compassion for the parents of infants born on the 7th, 17th and 27th. Unexpectedly, I received word that a dear friend back home had become the proud father of a first-born on July 27. It goes without saying that this family will need exceedingly careful help with a child who has some deep and critical lessons to learn, choosing, as it did, the last possible date in this century to incarnate for such a potentially intense experience.

Some Personality Examples   Curious as it might appear, Mozart, Beethoven and Kerry Packer have something special in

common: each has two 7s on his Birthchart. Each, in his chosen profession, has been through some severe lessons from which losses of a deep, personal nature have occurred. The first two, even though their lives were comparatively short, gained a deep level of personal understanding and spiritual awareness from their sacrifices. Kerry Packer is only now beginning to gain his.

With Mozart, losses in health and finances were the sacrifices he had to endure. In the life of Kerry Packer to date, losses have been largely to do with people, for he has experienced many acute disappointments and frustrations in his personal relationships. The other avenue of his sacrificing is indicated as his health — he must be especially careful as he approaches his next Personal Year 4 (in 1982), for this will be a year of exceptionally heavy demand on his nerves (see page 101). Beethoven's losses were in all three areas of human sacrifice — love, health and wealth. His two 7s of the Birthchart were compounded by his Ruling Number 7, resulting in Beethoven's life appearing as one of the saddest in the musical world. But to Beethoven the experiences were necessary and quite philosophically accepted. This is invariably the case with people in possession of multiple 7s in their numerology — their lives appear to be far sadder to observers. Deep within, people with multiple 7s recognise their need to learn by personal experience and they are not satisfied unless they have the freedom to so do.

THE NUMBER 8 ON THE CHART

This number exerts a somewhat unusual influence from its position at the end of the Spiritual (feeling) Plane. By symbolic representation, the 8 appears as the double 4, being one square atop another. This elevates some of the organisational and practical aspects of the 4 (along with some of its confining nature, if the person is living negatively) onto a higher plane of expression, as the following explanations reveal.

One 8   These people are usually most methodical and meticulous when living positively. On the other hand, apathy and instability prevail when they live negatively.

Tidiness, with considerable attention to detail and a feel for efficiency, is natural to those possessing one 8 on the chart. This orderliness combined with a perceptiveness which characterises the positive aspects of spirituality, gives them remarkable deductive ability.

If living negatively, these people will become restless and emotionally irritable, resulting in frequent changes of abode, job and interests. They must learn to stabilise and this can only happen with a positive outlook.

Two 8s   The sharpened power of assessment conferred by two 8s on the Birthchart can be either extremely beneficial or highly unsettling, depending on these people's command of positive thinking.

In matters demanding special care to detail, these people can excel like no others. But their perceptiveness must not be allowed to make them dictatorial from overconfidence. This would arouse emotional conflicts within them, thereby diluting their abilities and causing instability and restlessness.

These people will react to materialistic environmental circumstances by becoming unsettled. This is customarily expressed in their wish to travel, especially when young. If this desire is frustrated, it can lead to a feeling of confinement and uncertainty which could take years to dissipate. Travel can become their important lesson book and should be encouraged whenever possible because it will help them to gain equilibrium and eventually choose a life of peace.

Three 8s   This combination has occurred only three times each decade so far this century (in 1988 it will occur more frequently, of course). It is most unusual to meet such people, but if they are encountered we can be of particular help to them.

They must be made to realise that life is not pointless and frustrating once they amend their outlook. Until then they will be exceptionally restless.

For them, life really does not appear to begin until they enter their forties, by which time they appear to rapidly mature and establish a more balanced, positive outlook. Yet careful guidance can assist this change at a much earlier age, thereby allowing life to be much more rewarding for them.

Four 8s   Not since 1888 has a person been born with this intensity of 8s. (In that year a few were born with five 8s, and what restless lives they led!) It will occur again in 1988, during the month of August on the three days in which the number eight appears. As the science of numbers is independent of the limitations of time, here is some guidance for those to be born with this compounding.

They will invariably find an extreme restlessness impeding their progress in life and will have great difficulty applying themselves to a set job or to serious studies.

Until the turn of the century, they will want to be free to wander. It is best to let them do so, rather than induce frustration by confining them. They will begin to stabilise in their late teens or twenties.

Some Personality Examples
The admirable traits of attention to detail and of being methodical are shared, within our group, by three people who possess an 8 on their Birthcharts, and one who possesses two 8s. Napoleon Bonaparte, Caroline Jones and Sir Mark Oliphant are probably as diverse as it is possible for three famous people to be; yet they all have the strength of the single 8 on their Birthcharts. Thus, they evidence a methodical orderliness which has brought them considerable strength and benefits in their chosen professions. Whether soldier/ruler, reporter/interviewer or scientist/governor, meticulousness is a great asset.

By comparison Birthcharts with two 8s are rather rare. But when a person does possess them, we see evidence of an unsettled attitude to life. This proved so in the life of Lord Bertrand Russell, the famous British philosopher, historian and academic who achieved almost equal fame by turning his attention towards anti-government protests over policies which were unacceptable to his personal moral code. In his personal relationships he possessed a most penetrating perceptiveness which tended to make him appear overconfident, even dictatorial in his manner, especially with strangers. These are typical attributes of the double 8. His extensive travelling and the vehemence with which he protested his often radical viewpoints combined to ensure that Bertrand Russell achieved wide recognition. These expressions of his personality are related to his double 8 and his ruling 5, both of which are strengthened by his Arrow of Emotional Balance (Stage 7).

THE NUMBER 9 ON THE CHART

As the last number on the Mental Plane, at the same time being a number common to every person born this century, 9 exerts a strong influence over human affairs. It is the number of idealism and ambition. In classical mythology it is related to Mars, the god of war. This combination of influences has become very pronounced in the history of our century to date. Let us hope that man has now learned the futility of seeking to burden others with his ambitions and his ideals through acts of aggression.

One 9   Common to every birthdate in this century are the attributes of idealism and ambition to a degree previously unknown in the history of human life. Idealism and ambition have been the driving forces by which man has propelled himself into ever-expanding vistas of science and technology at a rate unknown since the height of the Atlantean cultural period 12,000 or more years ago. This is preparing mankind for the coming Aquarian Age (the new age of awareness, as many prefer to regard it); and as it draws closer, man will question more and more the reasons for his ambition and the chaos it has created. A considerable amount of culling will ensue.

The tendency to pursue the goal of high purpose for its own sake will diminish as the century nears its end and the universal awareness of the next millenium grows stronger. In time to come more wisdom will prevail in research and development, with harmony and environmental impact being vital considerations in determining what is appropriate to improve the quality of life.

Care must be taken to keep the reach for perfection in practical balance and not allow it to dominate to the point of fanaticism. We see examples of this obsessiveness today in the fervour of many environmentalists as they tend to overcompensate for previous environmental blunders. Hopefully the balance will soon be reached so that important ecological issues can be judged without emotional overtones.

Two 9s   An intensity of idealism and zeal, coupled with serious thought, characterises these people. But they must maintain careful balance in their ideas.

The inclination to become critical of others with a lower level of idealistic intensity must be watched and overcome if they are to find happiness in life.

In spite of their outward criticisms, these people are deep thinkers and really mean to be helpful. They must learn to express their intentions clearly and unemotionally, always guided by balanced practicality.

Three 9s   This exceptional power of idealism and ambition is extremely difficult to handle and can, at times, produce mental unbalancing.

Special care must be taken in the training of children with this aggregation of 9s because they relate everything too exclusively to the mental level.

It is not uncommon for small things to become mentally exaggerated out of all proportion, resulting in outbursts of temper which can be frightening to witness. These outbursts could precipitate loss of control that threatens mental balance.

A vital lesson here is to learn to look at things objectively, thereby developing a solid basis for comparison. This will improve the level of judgement and permit them to accept deviations from their rigid concept of the ideal.

Four 9s This combination occurs during three days (9, 19 and 29) of September during the last year of every decade in this twentieth century. We are, therefore, unlikely to meet many people born with this extreme concentration of mental power.

They will either live in a dream world of vague unreality or portray a somewhat belligerent attitude, unless they have mastered this great power and translated it into practical living.

As these people can easily become mentally unbalanced, they must be treated with the utmost patience and guided in a way which will allow them to express their alert mentality in practical terms. Guidelines for such can only be defined with an understanding of their Ruling Number and their name — from these we can recognise their purpose in life and how it is intended to be fulfilled.

Some Personality Examples

With the exception of Bertrand Russell, each of our twenty-five famous people is an example of the 9 on the Birthchart directing us along the path of idealism and/or ambition. Bertrand Russell also had these traits, even without a 9 on his Birthchart, for he had a Day Number 9.

Of special interest to us here are the characteristics revealed by the presence of three 9s on the Birthchart. Two of our personality examples have these — Germaine Greer and Bob Hawke. Both can be regarded as extremely idealistic, as evidenced by their public activities. One would perhaps hesitate to say that either is overly ambitious, except in their desire to support the causes for which they work. Bob Hawke's declared intent, at the end of 1979, to enter Federal politics might indicate a strengthening of personal ambition, for surely it could not be to gain personal recognition — he possesses more than any Australian now living. Perhaps this extra impetus derives from his Day Number 9. Even so, he must be careful that he does not overdo his ambitiousness, as already indicated in connection with his Ruling Number 6.

Germaine Greer is so wedded to the feminist cause that she has no time for any other personal ambition. As a ruling 7, with the Arrow of the Planner (page 83), she possesses an enormous capacity for promoting the ideals which are so precious to her. Her supportive literary successes and the deep seriousness which underlies her writings take much of their power from this formidable accumulation of 9s. But she must be especially careful to control her temper, for outbursts of rage will become mentally disturbing to her, possibly inducing her to lose credibility with those she seeks to convince.

The foregoing characteristics of individual numbers on the Birthchart form a reliable basic guide to the analysing of people's strengths and weaknesses. We are now in a position to undertake further development of the Birthchart so that a more complete picture will emerge. But first it is wise to gain a real understanding of the methods thus far developed by practising their application on our own birthdate and those within the immediate family. This will provide a better mental grasp of the method and the people involved. Please remember when practising self-analysis, that it should be undertaken objectively, recognising that we all have strengths and weaknesses, yet we all need to find balance. This can only be properly achieved when we know what we are doing and can see ourselves as we really are, not as we imagine ourselves to be.

You will find that, as you commence to use the foregoing system, your progress will be initially speedy. You will discover surprising new facts about your own and other people's personalities very quickly. Then you will reach a plateau. Gradually, as your intuition develops, you will achieve another break-through as the individual numbers of the Birthchart take on a new meaning. You will recognise in the Birthchart a formula, a pattern, so to speak, created by the impression of all the numbers working together to form a unique key to the personality under analysis. From then on, your expertise will develop amazingly.

STAGE 7
The Twelve Arrows on the Birthchart

It will be found in practice that where any three numbers exist in succession on the Birthchart a strength of special significance prevails. The presence of such an arrow throws an important light upon our knowledge of the Inner Self.

Another significant sequence we must consider is the absence of any three successive numbers from a line on the Birthchart, leaving a line of three empty spaces. These always highlight some of the lessons life intends us to comprehend, for they appear as weaknesses which must be balanced by whatever strengths we possess.

The expression "any three numbers" means a straight line series of either full numbers or empty spaces. Reference to the Birthchart will show that there are three vertical lines and three horizontal, of which any one or more can be full of numbers. There are also two diagonal straight line series, either or both of which can be full of numbers. This gives eight possibilities of full number straight lines. When we consider the possibilities of empty straight lines on the Birthchart, we find there are only four during this century — every birthdate will have a 1 and a 9 in the 1900s. Thus, mankind in general has potentially twice as many possibilities for additional strength (from the full lines), as for weaknesses (from the empty lines).

These twelve straight lines of full numbers or empty spaces, which we are now about to analyse, were named arrows by their most recent discoverer, Dr Hettie Templeton. It is quite likely that Pythagoras also used these arrows when numerologically analysing birthdates; however, their modern application had been overlooked by numerologists until the early 1930s. No other numerology book will be found to give such detail on this important series of traits, especially those related to children.

We should always give credit where it is due. And no one is due more esteem as a numerologist and counsellor than the late Dr Hettie Templeton. Born in Australia on March 25, 1887, Hettie Templeton struggled through her early life with a very large family and very little money or guidance. In her thirties, she discovered numerology through the teacher of a friend and was astounded at the assistance it gave her in rearing eight children. Twenty years later Hettie Templeton commenced to gain nationwide recognition as a competent numerologist. She lectured in Hawaii in 1938 and was again there in 1939 when she predicted the outbreak of the war in Europe for September of that year. Hettie Templeton was awarded a Doctorate in Science for her research into personality problems with children, a subject with which she had years of counselling experience. During the 1930s, she wrote two books on the science of numbers, the most famous, <u>Numbers and Their Influence</u>, undergoing numerous printings in Australia and the U.S.A. It was in this book that the Twelve Special Types of Charts, each identified by its particular arrow, were first published. The book is now out of print, but that introduction formed the basis of my own research and subsequent development of this important yet hitherto overlooked aspect of the science of numbers.

As we investigate the characteristics of each arrow, each will be defined by a key word. Special interpretation will also be given of the aspects of each arrow to help parents to better train and understand their children.

In most birthdates encountered at least one arrow will be found, if not of full numbers, then of empty spaces. Very often two, and occasionally three, arrows will be present in a birthdate. If they are arrows of full numbers, they usually indicate that the person being analysed has a strong character. But it is unwise to draw hasty conclusions in this work, for experience shows that many people achieve more with a limited chart than others who have much going for them. It is far more a case of what you do than what you have — of course, the combination of both is unbeatable.

As we consider each arrow, a birthdate will be chosen to illustrate it. In each case, care has been taken to ensure that the arrow appears in its simplest form, without any compounding of the numbers involved and without any other arrows to detract from the significance of that under consideration.

THE ARROW OF DETERMINATION

Birthdate of May 22, 1970:

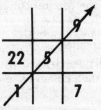

Everyone born in the 1950s has this arrow on his or her Birthchart. The consecutive diagonal numbers 1, 5, 9 on the Birthchart indicate the dominant traits of determination, persistence and endurance.

Determination underlies almost everything they undertake, coupled with a persistence and patience to overcome obstructions in executing their plans. If necessary they will wait until obstacles disperse. This is fine training for the development of endurance, but it could also prove futile. Sometimes stumbling blocks advise us that a planned course of action is unsuitable. If we heed that advice we could avoid later disappointment. Those who do not heed such indications can, after repeated frustration, become ruthless in their determination to have their way at all cost. This may give rise to cruelty which alienates others and ultimately rebounds upon themselves.

Determination must be combined with wisdom and awareness or its virtues will become vices. Moderation is a vital discipline for these people to embrace. If multiples of any number occur on this arrow, they will indicate the direction in which determination usually manifests. An accumulation of 1s will draw the determination towards ego and self-motivation; multiple 5s will increase the emotional intensity of the determination (often causing outbursts of temper from frustration); groupings of 9s increase idealism, ambition or demands of responsibility. If no 4 is present on the Birthchart the tendency towards impatience calls for extreme care and discipline in the presence of this arrow.

Children with the 1-5-9 arrow express very decided tastes with a strong spirit of determination, and need to feel free enough to express it. They should never be driven against their wishes, but need to be led with loving kindness and firmness, tempered by flexibility. Otherwise, they will be very hard to discipline, for they must be allowed opportunity to assert themselves.

Their determination strengthens them for their purpose in life and must not be confused with stubbornness. It gives them very decided likes and dislikes which they set about to satisfy. These are generally very intelligent children and can therefore be reasoned with. They will argue if the reasoning does not measure up to their level of logic and rarely do they hesitate to endeavour to make others understand them.

It is interesting to note that this spirit of determination gave rise to the emergence of the counter culture movement during the mid and late 1960s, when peaceful protests were successfully used to curtail the Vietnam war, the nuclear race and other ill-conceived counter-ecological activities.

Determination in Action   To attain positions of authority and leadership in their countries, politicians usually require a

considerable degree of personal campaigning. For this, they must possess strong persistence and determination. What a significant advantage politicians would have over their opponents if they were to possess the Arrow of Determination on their Birthcharts.

Such an advantage is shared by two current Commonwealth prime ministers — Malcolm Fraser and Margaret Thatcher. Both have reached their positions through relentless determination; both are poignant examples of endurance in action, for the fierce competition they encountered in their climb has thwarted many a less determined politician.

Birthcharts of both these prime ministers indicate confident self-motivation, encouraging them to undertake as much as they can physically and mentally handle. Their determination is directed by careful planning, for they also both possess the Arrow of the Planner (1-2-3). Both are noted for their determination to put into effect plans which they deem important, often in the face of severe opposition. The resourceful pair overcome resistance by adopting a variety of ploys.

Although the histories and geographical aspects of Australia and Great Britain are widely different, the two countries have more in common now than possibly ever before. One aspect of their present parallel is the conflict between their governments and their respective trade union councils. Both prime ministers appear committed to limiting what they consider to be too powerful trade unionism. It will be interesting to watch developments on this front, for if they are to succeed both prime ministers will need to employ all the resourcefulness and determination they can muster.

THE ARROW OF SPIRITUALITY

Birthdate of January 5, 1973:

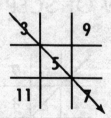

The arrow formed by the second diagonal on the Birthchart links the most powerful numbers on each of the three planes — the Mental 3, the Spiritual 5 and the Physical 7. This arrangement creates a deep spiritual awareness which is the vital basis for a balanced, practical philosophy of life. Such awareness encourages growth through personal experience because these people ordinarily do not heed advice from others. Where life's lessons are concerned, they much prefer practice to theory. This inclination will often bring sadness into their lives, inspiring fortitude and aiding the further unfolding of their philosophic understanding of life. Actually, their lives often appear sadder to the onlooker than is felt within themselves.

Experience brings them an inner serenity as they mature spiritually. It will often be said of them: "Their presence brings peace."

It is important to note that in this century every Birthchart with the Arrow of Spirituality also has the Arrow of Determination. Thus, the two should be read together for a more thorough understanding of these prominent traits.

Children with this arrow have an almost naive trust and deep sense of natural justice, so they must be carefully guided in spiritual (religious, philosophical and ethical) matters.

Parents must always be sincere and never anything but honest with these children. If not, they will undermine the children's trust and respect, which can often give rise to petty childish deceptions and dishonesties. This would be unsettling to them for they would be unaware of its cause — as often are the parents.

These children have a surprising ability for noticing what goes on about them, so strong are their powers of perception. However, their immaturity limits their ability to evaluate and express, tending to make many things in their young lives difficult to handle. Encouragement to read well-chosen books, instead of watching violence on TV, is especially helpful in developing their spiritual awareness and the understanding of their psychic faculties, such as intuition and E.S.P.

THE ARROW OF SCEPTICISM

Birthdate of April 2, 1968:

	6	9
2		8
1	4	

The absence of the numbers 3, 5 and 7 creates a diagonal arrow of emptiness. This generally indicates a scepticism towards anything metaphysical; yet these people emphatically embrace the more orthodox attitudes towards religion and science.

Although their feelings are no less loving and their sense of fairness no less just than those with the numbers 3, 5 and 7, the absence of these numbers indicates a more superficial understanding of human nature, creating occasional uncertainties. This gives rise to scepticism and worry often takes over. If allowed to magnify, worry causes headaches and other nerve problems (sometimes affecting the eyes and ears), of which these people often experience more than their share.

Worry and anxiety can cause unexpected reactions and lead to accidents in which the head will constantly figure. A sound philosophical understanding should be developed therefore realising that there is far more in life than can be recognised by man's five physical senses alone. This scepticism is best overcome by a developed sense of purpose which can lend meaning to life. There are many avenues by which this may be achieved. One of particular value is self-expression through art, writing or music.

If orthodox religion has, for any reason, disappointed these people, they tend to become agnostic in outlook. Again, any of the arts can help overcome this limiting attitude.

Children with this arrow express their scepticism in moodiness which can be trying to parents who do not understand. It is important for parents to realise that children with this arrow require peace and solitude. When anything upsets them they turn inward, finding in their isolation a means for retrieving mental and emotional balance.

When children are antagonistic the cause is often traceable to an inadequacy in their parents' expression of kindness and love. Parents must be loving, extremely patient, yet firm — at the same time encouraging their children in artistic participation to detract from influences beyond their present limits of understanding. If parents withdraw their love in reaction to the children's attitudes, a deep rift will develop between them which drives the children to spitefulness and aloofness.

Scepticism in Action
Bob Hawke and Sir Mark Oliphant are two famous people in whose Birthcharts the Arrow of Scepticism prevails. Neither man is unaware of his abilities for each has made his mark in his profession and gained worldwide recognition. Both men are involved in different aspects of the material world, one in human relationships, the other in the physical sciences, but both profess an orthodox outlook on human life and its purpose.

People with this arrow are inclined to deny the value of

intuition. Any hunch they might receive would not be accepted as of value until it had been tried, tested and conclusively proven to be worthy of application. Certainly this is the accepted approach of physical science and it is probably this tendency to be methodical which has raised Sir Mark to such a high level of academic recognition. He is at home with scientific or other orthodox procedures, but would be quite lost with metaphysical concepts. This matters little so long as he achieves satisfaction in his work and succeeds in bringing some small improvement to the quality of human life on this planet. (For those not prepared to accept metaphysical concepts on this Plane, adequate opportunity awaits in the ultimate realms of timelessness!)

Bob Hawke reveals a slightly different aspect of this arrow. A ruling 6, he is inclined to worry. This emotion is also associated with the Arrow of Scepticism, compounding its tendency to create headaches and extreme anxiety in Bob Hawke's life. His definite need is to adopt a deeper, more philosophical outlook — a requirement which his intuition has undoubtedly revealed to him long before now. In fact, we see some evidence of this outlook developing in his recent series as the 1979 Boyer lecturer. His new and refreshing approach to the philosophy of government has unmistakably precipitated his decision to enter federal parliament. But he must allow his philosophic studies a further advance, embracing, for instance, such profound principles as those developed by Pythagoras 2500 years ago when he too undertook the reformation of government but went even further — his reformation inculcated a completely new cultural epoch we now call 'western culture'.

THE ARROW OF INTELLECT

Birthdate of March 10, 1968:

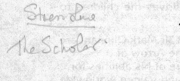

The presence of all three numbers on the Mental Plane indicates the importance of intellect and the dominance of mental activity in the expression of those with this arrow. Such a fertile intellect offers the potential blessing of a very good memory. Some people, however, will be found to possess this arrow on their charts and not exhibit a good memory — this undeniably implies laziness and wasted or abused talents.

People with this arrow show a preference for things intellectual and tend to ignore the importance of feelings (to what extent depends on their Ruling Number and the pattern of numbers on their Spiritual Plane). Surprisingly, they can be quite emotional without actually being aware of it.

There is a tendency for these people to become snobbish by seeking the company of only those people with high intellectual qualities and showing irritability towards those with lower IQs. They can master this by developing tolerance and compassion, realising that weaknesses are latent strengths yet to be made manifest. Life brings more responsibilities to these people than to most. But they handle their obligations well and are often happiest when performing duties for others. They are gregarious people who are rarely lost for words, but they tend to drive themselves to a point beyond natural tiredness. This is when their irritability becomes particularly noticeable. They must learn to balance mental and physical activity, with periods of relaxation and recreation.

Children with this arrow are, as a rule, brilliant at school, especially in mathematics and the analytical sciences. But their mental talents demand special tutorial care. They have very analytical brains, always investigating and planning, so these children should be given engaging and absorbing projects to suit them.

These children are inclined to be restive and headstrong, especially when they have insufficient to interest them. They respond well when called upon for assistance and appreciate praise for their efforts.

They must be always kept calm and never allowed to become over-stimulated. Should they become highly excited, their brains will slip into top gear and their thoughts run wild, pulling them in many directions at once. This could lead to hyperactivity if the diet contains sweets, white bread and preserved foods. Occasionally these children suffer from stuttering, fits and exhaustion due to over-stimulation.

They will detect attempts to deceive them and lose all confidence in the offender, for they are always analysing, evaluating and assessing.

Intellect in Action

When the Olympic Games commenced in 776 B.C. a gigantic impetus was given to sports, taking them out of the realm of disorganised games into the competitive arena of spectator engagements. Since then steady progress has been maintained in man's athletic challenge of the clock. With the advent of scientific method and its application to human activity, methods of sports coaching came under review. The new approach to athletic training led to the accelerated breaking of world sports records.

For most of this century, Australia has been a leading nation in many forms of athletics. In swimming we have been most successful, especially from the 1960s, and much of this success has been due to the creditable work of a former Olympic athlete, Forbes Carlisle.

Born June 3, 1921, Forbes Carlisle has a Birthchart with a most significant arrow, that of the balanced intellect. He is the only member of our group of twenty-five famous people with this arrow; but his life is one which exemplifies its characteristics conspicuously. In his own sports career, Carlisle achieved a remarkable level of personal discipline by his thoroughly intellectual approach to training. He rigidly adhered to his programme, irrespective of his bodily feelings. In fact, he almost drove himself to a state of irrecoverable exhaustion on more than one occasion. As a result of his own experiences, Forbes Carlisle developed a programme of training for swimmers from several months' old, right up to the age of competition in Olympic events. His methods embrace much more than physical training, including a total lifestyle consideration of diet, sleeping habits, drinking, smoking, etc. His plan is a total approach to athletics from a balanced, intellectual viewpoint. Also possessing the Arrow of the Planner, Forbes Carlisle had no problem in organising his methods into practical application. His entire numerological pattern, in fact, denotes balance, for he also possesses the two 1s, giving a balanced form of self-expression, and is a ruling 22/4, with the masterly balance between the practical and the spiritual aspects of life. Whatever he turned his hand to, Forbes Carlisle would make his efforts successful. We should be especially thankful that he has recognised the need to teach young people the life-saving activity of swimming and, with his wife Ursula, has devoted so many years to the organising of these classes.

THE ARROW OF POOR MEMORY

Birthdate of May 1, 1887:

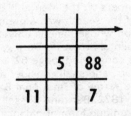

The absence of all three numbers from the Mental Plane is a rare phenomenon today. Everyone born since the beginning of 1889 possesses at least one number on this plane. Yet we include it in our lessons, for we are approaching the year 2000 and it is fascinating to speculate about twenty-first century man. The absence of these numbers does not imply that such people have no minds, but rather that their mental faculties are less active.

Unless they have been kept mentally stimulated, these people will suffer from a poor memory, commencing as forgetfulness but deteriorating to noticeable loss in later years. Life, then, seems very empty for them and they lapse into childish attitudes. They learn slowly and rarely rise to public prominence. Any exceptions are especially worthy of your investigation, for these people have mastered great handicaps and their lives should provide valuable lessons. Such people will appear quite witty and mentally alert — help having come through their Ruling Number, name and/or Sun Sign.

Children with this arrow will appear to be intellectually slow during their infancy and must be trained to concentrate and develop mental alertness. It is only a comparatively short number of years before infants will again be among us with Birthcharts containing this arrow. In anticipation of this book being available during that period, the following points will be of special importance.

Infant training must commence with creative interests, such as the arts and the sensitive awareness of nature. They should not start school early and should never be forced into academic study prior to the age of seven. Failure to observe this will invariably result in the children developing severe headaches, but these can be outgrown once the cause is recognised. Introducing academic studies to these children is a patience-demanding process. They are far more interested in natural phenomena and find the laborious training of

75

their memories tedious. Care and patience will win, so long as their interest is maintained.

Overcoming Poor Memory in Action
To find a person born prior to 1889 who has made a mark in the world and who possesses no numbers on the Mental Plane was not an easy task. The result of the search was a great surprise, for it uncovered a person whose fame is universally regarded as being based on mental prowess. Our example is Lord Bertrand Russell, whom we considered (page 62) when exemplifying the two 8s on the Birthchart, and shall consider again here, both for this arrow and the Arrow of Emotional Balance (which follows).

Born May 18, 1872, Bertrand Russell possesses a Birthchart which indicates a unique form of balance, yet is devoid of mind numbers 3-6-9. None could regard him as being of low intelligence; nor could he have achieved as much as he did without a better-than-average memory. So what gave him the intellectual prowess?

Whenever people achieve success in a field which apparently lies outside the powers indicated by their Ruling Number or their Birthchart, we must look at other aspects of their birthdate to discover under what influences they have tapped their power source. In our present example, we find that Bertrand Russell operated often under the power of his Day Number 9. Added to this is the mind power conveyed by his Sun Sign, being Taurus, and its proximity to the cusp with Gemini. These are strong mental influences and their power has been obviously effective for Russell. But they do not provide sufficient sustaining strength when the Ruling Number is so unhelpful and the Birthchart evidences such a handicap as this Arrow of Poor Memory.

Bertrand Russell was gaoled in 1918 for the pacifism he displayed during the Great War of 1914-18. It also cost his lectureship at Cambridge. This did not trouble him, for his strong emotional control (indicated by his Arrow of Emotional Balance) encouraged him to devote his efforts to his favourite activity, mathematics — while in prison he wrote his famous Introduction to Mathematical Philosophy. Bertrand Russell's title was an inherited one; his actions against many British governments would not have tempted them to flatter him with such recognition. When we look closely into the life of Bertrand Russell, we see many instances of mental unbalance and, as age overtook, a rapid decline in memory. These are to be expected with the absence of numbers on the Mental Plane and would have probably occurred earlier in his life were it not for his name containing so many mind numbers. 'Bertrand Russell' contains three 3s and three 9s, as well as a triple Arrow of

Determination. These were obviously powerful in his life's work, but were not strong enough to sustain him for the full duration of his years. Nonetheless, we can recognise, from this example, that no matter what numbers are missing from the Birthchart, their qualities can be developed by a judicious application of whatever strengths are present. This is how we achieve balance and grow that step closer to the ultimate purpose — the recovery of perfection.

THE ARROW OF EMOTIONAL BALANCE

Birthdate of August 2, 1965:

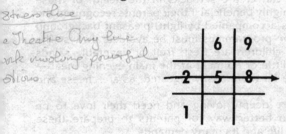

The completely full Spiritual (or feeling) Plane shows that these people have a natural balance in their emotional life and a depth of spiritual understanding which can be especially beneficial in this emerging new age of awareness. They see life as a balanced union of physical and spiritual elements, the former temporary and the latter permanent. It is this intensity of awareness which underlies their attitudes and which lends an air of constant seriousness.

They should seek bright company and the occasional pleasures of light entertainment to guard against becoming overly serious and withdrawn. They understand balance in spiritual terms but tend to overlook its wider expression, embracing as it does both the physical and the mental. This strong spiritual balance brings with it a natural healing ability which should be properly trained and developed. With fundamental coaching in anatomy, physiology, biochemistry, nutrition, etc., these people can be of inestimable benefit to mankind. Care must be taken that their training does not place too much emphasis upon dogmatic intellectual learning of such remote subjects as languages, formal logic and history. When they feel the need for these they will voluntarily embrace them. But in academic life such subjects would confuse, rather than assist, the natural healer.

Their balanced sensitivity helps them to perceive readily other people's points of view. This can be put to excellent use in their healing work since counselling is an intimate part of healing.

Children with this strong spiritual power can be so absorbed in their world of impressions that they are often regarded as dreamers. They are especially susceptible to emotional conflicts, preferring to withdraw than become involved. This tendency to withdraw is inclined to make them seem backward. Indeed it can hamper their early education. Parents should recognise the real cause and try to correct it, rather than express displeasure with the children. Some parents are selfish in this regard for, if the truth were told, they are more concerned about their own pride and family prestige than the welfare of their children.

Depth of feeling can create setbacks in the health of these children. It would be highly beneficial if their parents recognised the need for simple meals accompanied by light, pleasant background music. Noisy television programmes must be avoided always. The best foods for these children are fresh fruit or vegetable salads during the day, with little or no meat at the main evening meal — raw nuts or seeds are far more easily digested, as are cheese and eggs.

These children are deeply loving and need their love to be returned. There is no better way for parents to prepare these children to cope with life and its many demands.

During this century every Birthchart with this arrow will also possess the Arrow of Determination. These two major influences will either harmonise or conflict, dependent upon the overall pattern of the chart, the Ruling Number, given name and Sun Sign.

THE ARROW OF HYPERSENSITIVITY

Birthdate of June 9, 1971:

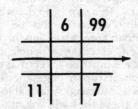

In contrast to the previous arrow, when no numbers appear on the Spiritual Plane of the Birthchart, problems of acute emotional sensitivity prevail. These people are so easily hurt, offended or upset in early years that they turn inward and become very shy. This creates an inferiority complex, causing them difficulty in social contact and a loss of trust. Most people outgrow this with maturity, overcoming it by steering conversations away from the personal, by achieving fame in some recognised field of endeavour, or simply by developing the practice of attack as their best line of defence. Nonetheless the absence of these numbers from the Birthchart implies an ultra-sensitive, tender and loving nature. They learn, usually by deep personal hurt, to become discriminatory in showing their feelings. Some rarely find happiness in love due to their manner of misrepresenting themselves.

Sometimes they appear stubborn, other times bold (to cover up their shyness), but always these people have an emotional vulnerability which few really understand or master. Yet emotional control is one of their important lessons in life and must ultimately be embraced.

Those who seek to overcome their hypersensitivity must first recognise the difference between reaction and positive action. They must cease being the victim of circumstances or reacting to others' opinions. Instead, let them learn to become the initiators, or the inspirers of endeavours. They will learn to recognise their strengths and use these to balance their personality and to achieve some measure of success in life. This gives them a basis for accomplishment and recognition. As a consequence, their understanding will grow and their faith in humanity be restored.

Children with these numbers missing are exceptionally shy and sensitive; yet with patience can be guided to overcoming the problem. Parents should recognise that the little tribulations in the mind of children with this arrow are very real and significant. They should take time to listen and give their love and encouragement generously.

These children crave love and seek every opportunity to serve those upon whom their love is centred. Thus, parents should always endeavour to find interesting little activities in which these children can help. And when they do a good job be sure to show approval and appreciation, for that is their manna from heaven. If these children do a job badly, or if they show anything short of perfection in anything else (for parents often expect perfection from their children), they ought not to be scolded or criticised in front of others. This is a certain way to entrench inferiority complexes and to lose the trust and respect of these children. Any chastisement or correction needed can always be given in private — and you may be assured that the message will be quickly recognised.

Hypersensitivity in Action
With this arrow appearing on the Birthcharts of four of our personality examples, we have some interesting observations to make regarding its relationship to the achieving of fame. Those under consideration are Joh Bjelke-Petersen, Indira Gandhi, Lang Hancock and Rupert Murdoch.

We have already looked into the erratic personality of Joh Bjelke-Petersen and discovered some of the reasons for his poor public image. Yet this image is not so unfavourable amongst the electors of Queensland, many of whom regard him as a sensitive, considerate person. Indeed, the presence of this arrow indicates he could be so, were he to learn to improve is self-expression.

The same can be said of Indira Gandhi. There is little doubt that she would command the largest pesonal following of any politician in India, yet the world's media appears to be in conflict with indigenous public opinion. She, too, appeared to have the interests of her country at heart, although from this distance we might easily take issue with her methods. But as we are not in her place, nor even in her country, are we in a fit position to judge? Of this there is no doubt; Indira Gandhi is an idealist (with her two 9s), has a strong personal ego (the five 1s), and is highly sensitive to her elected role. In fact, she shares most of these traits with Joh — 'what a pair', did someone say?

Lang Hancock might be said to have dug his way into fame with a shovel. His mineral discoveries have been primarily responsible for his national recognition. But wealth and 'luck' (as some would unthinkingly call it) are not the factors which have really brought this man into prominence. His wise and introspective comments about Australian attitudes and his recognition of the disastrous direction of business in this country are cogent and timely. They indicate a highly sensitive person, but one who, when he realises that insufficient people are interested or believe in what he says, closes up. This is the inner nature of a hypersensitive person. Let us not overlook that this man is a ruling 8 (that powerful number of strong commercialism and independence), has two 1s to give balanced self-expression and two 9s indicating a balanced and powerful idealism, combining with a 6 to give creativity and compassion. Indeed we should listen more to him.

As with those we have just considered, Rupert Murdoch (and most others possessing this Arrow of Hypersensitivity) has learned how to master his inner feelings as he attracts more publicity. The lack of these numbers of 'soul protection', or inner feeling control, implies only that these people are in very definite need of a lesson in emotional self-management. Once having achieved this discipline, they will find that many advantages await highly sensitive people, whether in business, politics or any other form of interpersonal relationship.

THE ARROW OF PRACTICALITY

Birthdate of February 6, 1974:

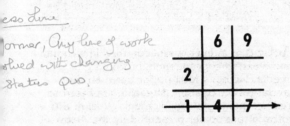

With all numbers of the Physical Plane present on their Birthchart, the basic outlook is one of intense practicality. The best expression of these people will always be related to the physical which, in many cases, means materialism.

These people are usually clever with their hands, but just which direction their talent should take them is best indicated by their Ruling Number. If this Ruling Number is 4, 7 or 10, their emphasis towards the material is strengthened, for it is here that their purpose has to be fulfilled. With the Ruling Number of a spiritual or mental vibration they will rise above material limitations and may become capable artists or musicians. Although they are kind and ever ready to help others, this heavy physical emphasis makes for poor judges of character.

Often they are motivated by worldly desires, unless intensely involved in creative work. Care should be taken that they do not become too caught up in the material but, rather, learn to utilise their power in a constructive way, either as tradesmen or organisers.

Children with this vibration exhibit a strong desire for material things, yet are much happier being with nature and learning to appreciate the higher qualities of life. They are apt to take things for granted, so the virtue of appreciation and the value of sharing should be encouraged in them.

These children should never be forced into activities they do not like. Kindness will always win the day with them and they will not object to physical tasks, for that is where they feel most capable. Unreasonable insistence will only arouse in them resentment which could develop into obstinacy. If this occurs often it might lead to an attitude of destructiveness which can be exceedingly harmful to themselves and others. To avoid their mixing with children who might already be of a disruptive nature, parents should exercise great wisdom — but it must be done subtly. Little friends with gentle natures, such as those children who appreciate and enjoy being with nature and who love to share things, make their best playmates.

Never bribe with money or gifts because the aim should be to direct their thoughts away from the material. Love and appreciation are by far the best rewards.

Practicality in Action

If ever we needed evidence that a woman could become extremely capable in business or influential in the media, we need look no further than the editor of Australia's largest circulation magazine. Ita Buttrose has directed the rise of <u>The Australian Women's Weekly</u> with a talent which is typical of the power presented by the Arrow of Practicality, especially when related to as strong a Ruling Number as her 7. This arrow is the only strength of significance indicated on the Birthchart of Ita Buttrose, but its power has provided the impetus she needed to undertake the enormous challenge which justifies her inclusion in this list of exemplary people. She is determined to maintain her magazine in the forefront of circulation figures and, in this direction, has added strength from her name with its Arrows of Determination and of Intellect. Coupled with these powers are her Day Number 8, her Capricornian nature and the general balance to her Birthchart given by her name chart.

As far as domestic chores are concerned, it would be hard to believe she had the inclination for them, yet there is no doubt that she has very definite ideas as to what should be done and when, what should be put where and how. But her concerns are of a material nature, in accordance with her powerful ambition.

To a large extent, Ita Buttrose is a lone worker. She prefers to be the ruler of her domain and does not readily accept anyone else into it. But she is successful and, because of that, she is allowed free rein. With this freedom, she will grow in strength so long as she recognises the guidance offered by her intuition and does not take things too much for granted. In her position she is especially vulnerable to health problems arising from a highly acid-forming diet. Any Capricornians involved in business entertaining are inclined to suffer so.

THE ARROW OF THE PLANNER

Birthdate of August 2, 1943:

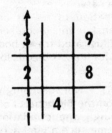

Due to the myriad occasions on which the numbers 2 and 3 occur together in birthdates, this arrow is one of those most frequently found. Joining, as it does, the initial numbers on each of the three planes, the first vertical arrow brings with it the special quality of adroit planning. Some numerologists regard this arrow as one of thought power, but it is more than that. It reveals a unique combination of thought, intuition and personal expression, giving rise to many inspired plans, varying from those of little importance to many of significant consequence.

An inherent love for order, method and the scheme of things is present here. However, the planner prefers to concern himself more with organisation than with practical details. If his Ruling Number is 4, 7, 10 or 22/4, or if he has a 4 or 7 on the Physical Plane, this tendency is greatly minimised; otherwise, it could develop into laziness. With such excellent capacities as planners, these people must guard against the temptation to overlook the importance of the smaller things in life, such as giving small tokens of appreciation, consideration of others' feelings and those little kindnesses which are often thought about but rarely expressed.

Children with this arrow are also happiest when organising some little plan of their own, but often this runs counter to the plans of their parents, causing disappointments which only love and patience from the parents will help them to understand.

In their planning world, these children are inclined to be detached and to take much for granted, so involved are they in their own thoughts and schemes. This detachment causes an aloofness which often results in unawareness of others' needs. Loving but firm discipline is needed to teach them the need for co-operation. They should never be bullied or threatened, but instead gently taught to respect the ideas, possessions and habits of others.

83

These children have a trusting, gentle nature and are often slow to realise when injustices have been perpetrated upon them. This naivete is charming, but could make them gullible until they get hurt often enough to realise that not everyone is as guileless as they.

There is sometimes a nervous restlessness in their earlier years, resulting from the inclination to reflect and speculate, but not knowing quite how to translate this mental energy into the physical. Encouragement to read illustrated travel books is an excellent way of satisfying this feeling, for it absorbs this love of investigating and exploring the unknown.

Planning in Action
Not surprisingly, the Arrow of the Planner is one found on the Birthcharts of many successful people because planning is the foundation of success in life.

Planning has become such a vital activity in the life of Richard Bonynge that we shall use his birthdate as our example. Born 9-29-1930, he has become one of the most recorded orchestral conductors of the 1960s and 70s. His strict ideals of musical expression are based on the power of the three 9s on his Birthchart. His highly creative expression derives its power from his Ruling Number 6. These attributes would be of little value without the talent to plan them into production. This Bonynge does with great skill, thanks to the well-balanced arrow formed by the numbers 1-2-3 on his Birthchart. However, the one 1 does not give him the ideal balance in his verbal self-expression, causing him to prefer to express himself through music to avoid misunderstandings. Occasionally he finds himself being severely misunderstood and often makes statements he wishes afterwards he could retract. More use of his planning ability will minimise this. By putting as much planning into his verbal expression as he does into his musical he will learn to think carefully before making a strong comment.

THE ARROW OF THE WILL

Birthdate of April 5, 1968:

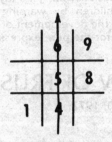

The vertical line created by the three numbers running up the centre of the Birthchart links the physical with the creative. Its presence represents the power of the will, the force by which thought is translated into action, symbolising the spine and the life force (Kundalini) which ascends it. Abundant activity and strong will-power are embodied here. When these traits are combined with determination (because of the presence also of the 1-5-9 arrow), we find the makings of very dynamic people.

So intent are these people on pursuing their courses of action that they can become oblivious of the feelings and wishes of others. This tendency arises from their strong desire for personal involvement, although it is sometimes mistaken for disinterest. Misunderstandings of this nature arise from breakdowns in communication — the result of their taking the concurrence of others for granted without consulting them or without the guidance of their own intuition. Often strong willpower can override instinctive knowledge if the two are in conflict. This will occur from time to time for those possessing this powerful arrow. These strong-willed people must learn to place more faith in the guidance of their intuition.

Children with this arrow are also very strong-willed, but their greatest pleasure is derived from expressing themselves in deeds of kindness. They must be trained to understand other people's points of view and accept guidance so that their kind deeds are beneficial to others. There can be a tendency towards self-interest which, if allowed to gain control, can lead to acute stubbornness. Parents must guide these children with patience, love and understanding. Never push them or impatiently command them, for this would only increase their stubbornness and cause continual clashes of will.

As well as prompting these children to be thoughtful, parents

85

must always show appreciation with loving praise. This carries far more weight than any other form of appreciation. Too often parents resort to the easy and quick way of showing approval or giving encouragement — bribes of sweets, money etc. This is a guaranteed recipe for spoiling children by warping their sense of values, frequently resulting in the development of very mercenary natures. There is no substitute for the pure expression of love.

THE ARROW OF FRUSTRATIONS

Birthdate of January 20, 1972:

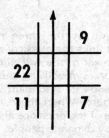

In the post-war years of the 1940s, 1950s and 1960s birthdates with this arrow of emptiness did not occur. The presence of this arrow applies only to some people born before the end of 1939, or since the beginning of 1970. The arrow indicates a divided Birthchart; the absence of numbers 4, 5 and 6 from the birthdate reveals some special lessons to be experienced. Absence of all numbers from the Will Arrow implies the need to strengthen the ability of conscious and deliberate action, the willpower. The absence of these numbers does not indicate lack of will, but rather a reluctance or hesitancy to act purposefully.

These people often expect more from others than they themselves are prepared to give. Expectation is a basic cause of frustration. We should realise that frustrations could be avoided if only we learnt to appreciate people for what they are, rather than what they can be or should be. No-one is everything they could be because we are all in a state of evolving. Personal growth is very slow and can never be forced. Accord to everyone the respect to which they are entitled for the progress they have made thus far — such appreciation is the best encouragement for further development.

Life has many different ways of ensuring that its lessons are learned. People with this arrow are aware that the various losses, separations and disillusionments life presents to them (and there can be quite a few), are vital steps in their evolution. They often experience great disappointment in others, from which they must develop an understanding of the reasons for life's many trials. Until this awareness develops they feel sad, and sometimes lonely and dejected. Such people can derive immeasurable benefit from studying and applying the science of numbers to their lives.

Children with this arrow need special love and attention, for life to them can often seem unfairly victimising. Disappointments in their friends and loss of faith in others can cause them to lose confidence in themselves. This creates moods of dejection which they do not understand.

Parents must be especially careful to maintain a strong bond of friendship with these children and never do anything which could undermine their trust. It should be understood that their moodiness comes from feelings of betrayal and, if called upon to explain themselves, they could be drawn into depths of depression from which they might take days to emerge. Patient understanding and almost limitless love from the parents will provide the bulwark by which these children will regain confidence in themselves and faith in other people.

Overcoming Frustrations

Experience shows that it is a matter of what you do with what you have, rather than what potential is available to you to create a success of your life. This is illustrated well by the lives of our twenty-five famous people. Not one of them has the Arrow of the Will, yet ten of them possess the Arrow of Frustrations.

It would be generally thought of people who have achieved a significant level of fame that they possessed a high potential in terms of personality traits but often this is not the case. It appears that those with the greatest challenges to overcome will succeed by employing the strengths they possess to balance out their weaknesses, whereas those with a ready-balanced Birthchart of considerable potential strength often do little with it.

The Arrow of Frustrations divides the Birthchart into two and implies that only intense personal application will see plans carried through into actions. As this purposefulness is practised with increasing success, greater encouragement attends continued perserverance. This is the recipe for success for people whose Birthcharts embrace this arrow, as we see in the lives of Joh Bjelke-Petersen, Richard Bonynge, Indira Gandhi, Germaine Greer, Bob Hawke, Caroline Jones, Senator Edward

Kennedy, Rupert Murdoch, Sir Mark Oliphant and Kerry Packer.

Germaine Greer is extremely responsive to this arrow. With no help from her Ruling Number or her Day Number, and only a little help from her Name Numbers, she typifies a life in which many varied frustrations play a continual role. This could be a primary factor in determining her attitude towards what she regards as sexual inequality.

By contrast, Rupert Murdoch, with the same Arrow of Frustrations, has the power of adaptability conferred by his Ruling Number 10 to enable him to adjust readily to circumstances which might otherwise become extremely frustrating. We see this in action in his various attempts at corporate raiding — in some he is spontaneously successful, but often he meets with considerable frustrations which cause him either to abandon the attempt entirely or to make a later one. He no doubt regards these frustrations as ideal opportunities to reassess his position. That indeed is their purpose and it would save many disappointments in people's lives would they but realise this.

THE ARROW OF ACTIVITY

Birthdate of June 8, 1972:

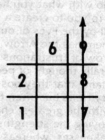

The last full arrow on the Birthchart is composed of the three numbers .joining the most expressive aspects of each of the horizontal planes. The combination of higher learning by sacrifice with perceptiveness (the 8) and ambition (the 9) can cause hyperactivity. In children hyperactivity is easily vented in spontaneous physical expression, but adults use more restraint, preferring to suppress their actions, resulting in nervous irritability.

Man is by nature an expressive creature. This arrow on his Birthchart indicates a higher than average desire to express himself through action. The constraints of modern society conspire to inhibit his freedom of expression to such an extent that he becomes agitated by the accumulation of suppressed nervous energy. The result is often extreme nervousness which may induce any number of illnesses, including asthma, diarrhoea, headaches, migraine, hypertension, strokes and toxemia. Social disturbances, such as arguments, are particularly distressing to these people. Peace and harmony are necessary to their constitutions and for this reason they should spend as much time as possible with nature. They are not happy city dwellers. On the contrary, they often find the tensions of the city to be most stress-inducing.

The desire to commune with nature and to be active implies the enjoyment of bushwalks, hiking, farming, gardening and any sports or activities requiring plenty of fresh air and open space. Pure, natural foods are vital ingredients in the diets of these people. Their digestive systems do not take well to processed or highly seasoned foods, preferring instead simple fresh fruits and vegetables, nuts, seeds and grains. Pure foods and plenty of outdoor exercise are the best medicines, in fact the only ones to which these people will unfailingly respond when enervation overtakes them.

It is important for highly active people that their thoughts be uplifted to noble levels. They should attempt to improve their expression through writing, especially on subjects related to the wonders of nature.

Children with this arrow are especially susceptible to high levels of noise, demanding peace, love and harmony in all they do and wherever they go. Being highly excitable and impressionable they demand the outdoors and always should be allowed to commune with nature. If possible they should sleep, eat and play out of doors, for this will give their high level of activity far more scope for expression and will calm their emotions.

Noisy or disturbed conditions can cause serious setbacks to the schooling of these children, as well as impeding their social adjustments. Their great need is for peace and anything short of this will interfere with their mental and emotional dispositions. Special care must be taken if exposing them to television to avoid violent, suspense and thriller programmes. They will be far happier and healthier if they can totally avoid that square-eyed monster.

Early bed at night is important for these children; so too is harmony in the home. There must not be arguments and tension, else serious health problems with arise, even if the children are not directly involved in the conflicts. The mysterious infantile disease known to result in cot deaths can often be traced to psychic disturbances which prevented the development of adequate harmony between the soul and its new body. Such problems would be far more serious to infants with this arrow because they are ultra-sensitive to disharmony and noise.

Activity in Action
There are two distinct aspects of activity indicated by this arrow both of which stem from the normal desire to be expressive. The most natural is the desire to feel free, to feel the limitlessness of the gigantic space which surrounds us. This maintains personal calmness and a state of permanent peace and contentment. But this is often far from possible in this hectic world. The second aspect of activity comes into being when the first is frustrated. It is then recognised as hyperactivity, resulting from the suppression of personal freedom. The body seeks to rebel, leading to all sorts of curious actions.

Prince Philip tends to conform to the first aspect. This is not seen in his Birthchart, but in his name (see Stage 12). We have already recognised him as a peace-loving man with a strong family love, but when we analyse his name, we find that 'Philip' is almost totally along the Arrow of Activity. (Sharing this name, but with an additional 'l', the author is very aware of its power in this direction!) When related to his ruling 2, we can see why this man will always seek the peaceful approach, yet enjoy the freedom of being able to express himself physically.

By contrast, the Birthchart of Napoleon Bonaparte, with its Arrows of Activity and of Determination is a classic example of the second aspect of the arrow which is recognisable as hyperactivity. History indicates to us that he was a man who must have suffered many frustrations in expressing himself physically during his earlier life. His later actions were consistent with a disturbed nervous condition resulting from extreme suppression. That this led him to conquer huge tracts of land confirms that he felt constricted, becoming so exhilarated with his initial successes that he did not know when to stop — a common symptom of hyperactivity. His strong determination fueled his enthusiasm for expansion, but at a heavy penalty to his nerves and with frequent illnesses. Napoleon enjoyed the outdoors but millions suffered at his pleasure.

STAGE 8
The Day Numbers—Your Other Self

Throughout all life we find balance, and, in the absence of balance, the effort to restore it. Winds are created to balance atmospheric air pressures; night and day permit man's energy balance to be effected between rest and activity; and karma creates the balance between what we actually do and what we should do.

Human personality also has its balance in the grand scheme of things. We know that man is intended to discover his singular pathway in life and to grow in that direction by personal experience. That is life's purpose. But we must also recognise that he is not intended to proceed in that direction unremittingly without some balancing periods of controlled diversion. Without these man could become so intense that his nervous energy would be exhausted early in his lifetime. As a result, a state of mild monomania could develop from his obsession with growth and progress. In extreme cases, man could become so preoccupied with his progress as to cause premature disability. This would totally negate his real aim: to develop an understanding of his sensitive, eternal being, the Inner Self. For this a strong, alert attitude is necessary.

Intimately related to our studies of the Inner Self is our understanding of the expression of the outer self, the personality. Our understanding of the Ruling Numbers and the numbers of the Birthchart gives us an excellent outline of a man's basic personality. So let us now look at his diversionary personality, his other self, to enable the complete picture to be developed.

Most, though not all, people have this diversionary aspect clearly indicated in what we call the Day Number. The Day Number, however, offers a variation of influence when it differs from the Ruling Number, as will be shown to occur with the vast majority of birthdates. Some people possess the same Day Number as Ruling Number. Their need to strengthen their Ruling Number is obviously greater than the need to divert from it.

The Day Number, in its preparation for analysis, is regarded in the same basic manner as the Ruling Number. Each double number of a day on which a person is born is resolved to a single number by

91

simple addition, except in those instances when a person is born on the 10th, 11th or 22nd day of the month. These numbers maintain similar properties to those we found when considering their Ruling Number counterparts.

The only Day Number which does not exist as a Ruling Number is the number 1. A person born on the first day of the month has the Day Number of 1. This is analysed differently to the Day Number of 10 ascribed to those born on the 10th, 19th or 28th day of the month. To ensure we know exactly what Day Number applies to each day of the month, here is a checklist:

Day Number 1 — persons born on the 1st day of any month;

Day Number 2 — persons born on the 2nd or 20th day of any month;

Day Number 3 — persons born on the 3rd, 12th, 21st or 30th day of any month;

Day Number 4 — persons born on the 4th, 13th or 31st day of any month;

Day Number 5 — persons born on the 5th, 14th or 23rd day of any month;

Day Number 6 — persons born on the 6th, 15th or 24th day of any month;

Day Number 7 — persons born on the 7th, 16th or 25th day of any month;

Day Number 8 — persons born on the 8th, 17th or 26th day of any month;

Day Number 9 — persons born on the 9th, 18th or 27th day of any month;

Day Number 10 — persons born on the 10th, 19th or 28th day of any month;

Day Number 11 — persons born on the 11th or 29th day of any month

Day Number 22/4 — persons born on the 22nd day of any month.

Now that you have checked your own day of birth and noted your Day Number, you will be ready to discover what part it plays in your life and how it influences your personality. But first a few interesting points should be explained.

The Day Number will always be found to possess similar properties to the Ruling Number, although at a lower level of strength. This is an important consideration, for since the role of the Day Number is that of guide to man's other self, it should never be regarded as indicative of the actual Pathway a person is intended to follow (which is more correctly revealed by the Ruling Number).

Around one in every twelve people possesses the same Day Number as Ruling Number. Realising nothing happens by chance, we must seek the reason for this occurrence. It is to be found in that person's apparent need for additional strengthening in his personality to enable him to more successfully fulfil his purpose in life and to overcome exceptional challenges on the Path. With the strengthening of the intensity of the Ruling Number comes a reduction in any diversionary aspects of this person's personality to the point that such diversion primarily must derive from changes in the Personal Year Numbers. These we shall analyse in the following stage.

Let us now look at the general characteristics indicated by each Day Number to understand how they influence the personality.

Day Number 1   People born on the first day of each month always do their best when allowed to work on their own. They require ample freedom to best express themselves and to permit maximum scope for the development of their initiative. The direction in which this expression is best achieved is indicated by their Ruling Number, although they will sometimes depart from this direction and become involved in some diversionary project for a limited period. This is their release valve. Because of their preference for individual effort, these people might seem to become aloof or detached for certain periods — this will be especially noticeable in children, and should cause no alarm for it is merely their other self enjoying its seclusion.

Day Number 2   The effect of this Day Number is to induce a desire to work closely with someone who has a bright, happy disposition. It also attracts towards light entertainment, especially if humorous. These people most certainly prefer to be entertained than do the entertaining. They are light-hearted, happy people, preferring the natural to the artificial.

Day Number 3   Here we have the part-time entertainers — the people who thoroughly enjoy all forms of humour, especially satirical humour. They are generally bright extroverts with an active brain and a ready answer. There is an underlying tendency to be critical of more sombre people, without attempting to understand the nature of these different personalities. Care should be taken to resist this destructive urge and to be more helpful to such people by introducing a little light-hearted, impersonal humour into their lives.

Day Number 4   A practical and capable flair helps these people to express themselves with their hands or feet. If their Ruling Number is an odd number this Day Number will be especially beneficial in creating balance with that predominantly artistic or philosophical approach to life. Should the Ruling Number be an even number, they must take care to avoid an undue emphasis on materialism, learning to achieve best efficiency from their actions with a balance between what is needed and what they wish to see achieved. It is especially important to exercise such control if the Ruling Number is 4, 8 or 10, due to the strong element of materialism and commercialism possible there.

Day Number 5 The general characteristic of the Ruling Number 5, the seeking of freedom, prevails almost as strongly in this Day Number. It creates in these people the desire to openly express their feelings. Yet they often refrain from so doing for any number of imagined reasons, such as shyness and fear of being misunderstood. Unless they become more unreserved and act more naturally, they could develop an inner intensity, an uptightness, with all its attendant nerve-oriented problems.

Day Number 6 The creativity with which the 6 is typically associated finds its particular expression as a Day Number centred in the home. When applied in a positive, constructive manner, this number strengthens the feeling for love and beauty in the immediate environment, whether it be home, office or work area. Negatively expressed, the Day Number 6 brings with it an over-dramatisation of domestic problems and all sorts of fears, worries and dreary complaining — in short, people whom most of us would try to avoid.

Day Number 7 The special purpose of this number is to induce a degree of personal involvement in experiences intended to instill a deeper set of values. These lessons provide vital training which, for many people, is only of value when it affects the pocket, the heart or the health. Most frequently it is the pocket, for money is the commodity upon which most people base their values. The quicker they learn by such lessons the more temporary will be their effect and the more progress they will make in understanding their lives.

Day Number 8 People tend to work and act as part of a group, so accustomed are they to being organised and directed. This does not help to develop independence, however. When people have a Day Number of 8 it indicates their need for periods of independence, varying from occasional to frequent intervals, depending upon their Ruling Number and the degree to which their awareness has developed. Some self-direction is vital to the development of higher self through awareness. Such periods should not be utilised, as some tend to, merely for developing monetary independence, for this is lopsided. Often financial security comes as a natural consequence of attaining a high degree of self-awareness through mental independence.

Day Number 9 The level of expression for this Day Number is the mental. All who possess it discover that, from time to time, their efforts are directed towards an idealistic improvement of human life. Consequently, their own level of responsibility is increased. In turn this benefits their personal development but it must not be mistakenly limited to personal ambition. Ambition is a noble trait when exercised with wisdom and directed towards the common good, but when directed toward selfish gain it becomes a savage taskmaster, leading to dissatisfaction, aggressiveness and possibly mental unbalance. People with a Day Number 9 should select their priorities carefully, avoiding enslavement to an unbridled ambition.

Day Number 10   The power of adaptability characterised by the Ruling Number 10 is seen here in a more superficial expression. People with a Day Number 10 are gregarious, energetic and easy to please, usually immensely liked by those who meet them. But they have a tendency to be superficial, sometimes to the point of inconsiderate glibness. They must avoid wasting their lives by recognising that the purpose of this Day Number is to balance their more serious side. The Ruling Number will always direct their higher development, while the Day Number is merely intended for occasional relief.

Day Number 11   The high level of spirituality with which this number is identified usually finds expression on the emotional level as a Day Number. It brings with it a degree of intuitiveness well above the average, but unless those with a Day Number 11 have learned how to handle it they could become involved in emotional extremes. This occurs if they have not developed adequate self-mastery, the result being wildly fluctuating moods. If not controlled such nervous demands will exhaust the body, leading to an enervated condition and depleted health. This will significantly contribute to premature old age. Yet when these people have mastered their emotions the power of this Day Number is extremely valuable in their intuitive development.

Day Number 22/4   The power of this number is second to none. Its influence as a Ruling Number is dynamic and only slightly diminished when it appears as a Day Number. The power felt by those whose Day Number is 22/4 often induces them to rely upon it, rather than living their Ruling Number. This creates problems for they do not possess the inner sustenance to live at this pace, as do those with the 22/4 Ruling Number. Under such circumstances the power of this Day Number is fragmented between its physical and spiritual counterparts: materialism and the spirit of love. This produces an imbalance which they find difficult to comprehend, especially if their Ruling Number is an even one and particularly a 2, 4 or 10. Until they have firmly planted their feet upon the Path (as indicated by the Ruling Number) the strength of the Day Number

22/4 will not be channelled beneficially. For this reason it is of the utmost importance that they learn to balance the physical and the spiritual aspects of life.

It is important to remember that your Day Number is the key to your other self. It should never be relied upon as the primary Pathway. Those who have attempted to do that have placed themselves in a state of confusion, uncertain of their direction and of what life holds for them. This has resulted in many cases of mental and emotional instability.

Often people are motivated by desires which have been stimulated by their reactions to other people, to advertisements, to unrequited appreciation or love, or to any number of emotional factors. By so reacting, they are no longer themselves and often flip over to adopting the alternative characteristics of their Day Number. Here we see the root cause of many cases of instability which has created discontented and unhappy lives. I have often lamented the ignorance evidenced by those in charge of mentally handicapped and mentally deranged people of this highly reliable method of getting to know the inner world of the patient. The understanding of the personality, and of the qualities shown by the Ruling Number and the Day Number, provide invaluable guidance in how to treat the patient. Not only is the personality symbolised correctly by the numbers, but when this system is regularly used it will produce an ever-increasing development of the practitioner's intuition so that the innermost desires, motivations, fears and even karmic influences of the patient are revealed.

STAGE 9
The Personal Year Numbers— Your Cycle of Change

'There is a tide in the affairs of men,
Which, taken at the flood, leads on to fortune.'
William Shakespeare.
(Julius Caesar, IV, iii)

From Stage 8 we have seen that most people possess diverse aspects to their personality. These are required to balance their individuality to more successfully fulfil their purpose in life. But there is another important variation for us to consider now. Although not related directly to the personality, it is directed to the same end — the achieving of one's purpose. This phase is the cycle of the Personal Year Numbers.

We have all found that some years of our lives stand out for their exemplary progress, others for their time-consuming frustrations. Our memory seems to cling to these extremes. Were the memory more reliable and more cognisant of other than extremes we would also recall other years of stabilising quietude when no material progress or frustrations of discernible note occurred. We would have also detected cycles of change running through our lives. These cycles allow an important balancing in overall growth. There are, in fact, cycles of change in the life of every person which can be readily analysed, recognised and applied to each year through which we pass while on earth. (These can, of course, only occur while we are in the physical body, for it is only while we are a part of these earthly vibrations that time, as we know it, prevails.)

Once we arrive at this point of recognising our cycles of change we shall become aware of their purpose and act more wisely in co-operating with them. These changes are necessary to allow man suitable periods for growth on each of his three vital levels — physical, spiritual and mental. These must always be followed by periods of stabilisation during which the preceding period of development can be properly assimilated.

These cycles are not haphazard occurences. They are very carefully planned, as is everything in nature. By our recognition of them we become more aware of the divine plan of life, learning not to expect every year to be one of dynamic progress and material gain. If we come to recognise each year for its particular purpose we can select our activities in accordance with our need for physical, spiritual or mental development. More progress is always achieved by swimming with the current than by fighting against it.

Why should such cycles of change occur in human life? In true Socratic manner, the reply is: Doesn't everything on earth, even earth itself, move in accordance with planned cycles; so why not man? Divine order regulates the universe — nothing and no-one is excepted. In strict compliance with divine order, growth, i.e. evolution, takes place in spiralling, ever-opening cycles. The twenty-four-hour cycle embracing day and night is designed to facilitate alternate growth and rest over a comparatively short period. The four-season year facilitates growth and rest in a larger cycle. Both cycles, we know, are governed by the sun and that, too, has cycles of change in its intensity.

This astronomical abode we call earth has its annual cycles as well. Its years of change will come to be recognised as following the same pattern as the nine-year cycle which applies to human evolution. Every nine years a complete cycle is made with changes occurring each year within the cycle, following a pattern of analysable variation. For man and his planet the nature of the influence of each year is symbolised by successive year numbers. For man these are called Personal Year Numbers; for the planet, they are known as World Year Numbers. Let us first take a look at the pattern of World Year Numbers.

We must, of necessity, concentrate our studies upon our calendar system, but we will have no difficulty interpreting other calendar cycles if we so desire. We know that all numerical systems of time measurement are in harmony with each other and with those they have succeeded. With our own system of numbers (which, happily, is employed by the vast majority of countries), we find that the nine-year cycle continues relentlessly through this current (or Christian) era in exactly the same manner as it does in the older Roman, Greek and Hebrew calendars. There is a slight variation of meaning in the numbers, but this is to be expected when we consider the modification in lifestyles, attitudes and consciousness brought into being with the advent of Christianity.

Analysing World Year Numbers alone provides an interesting exercise, but they will not tell us very much about the world on their own. We can readily see that the year 1979 was an 8 $(1 + 9 + 7 + 9 = 26/8)$, but of far stronger influence on world affairs are the Ruling Numbers and Personal Year Numbers of national and international political, financial or cultural leaders. Only when we undertake a deep analysis of world trends involving detailed analyses of world leaders would we consider it worthwhile analysing the World Year Number and setting up the chart of each year to ascertain the influence it plays on world trends. But as it is an influence only, and not a cause, we shall not delve into it in this book, for our primary interest lies with the Inner Self.

The Personal Year cycle of nine years commences for each person on the day of birth. Your Personal Year Number for that year is the same as your Ruling Number. But your Ruling Number remains constant throughout your life, although its influence is modified somewhat when you come onto the Pyramids (Stage 10). However, variations in your thinking and in your emotional and material influences follow a pattern of cyclic change of nine-year duration. These cycles are readily analysed. We calculate our Personal Year Numbers by reducing the individual numbers of our birthday in the year under consideration.

As an example birthdate, let us again use April 21, 1926, for it belongs to one of the best known and best loved people in the world, Queen Elizabeth II. To calculate her Personal Year Numbers over this decade we shall list the dates of each of her birthdays, commencing with her year of birth, then jumping to 1971.

April 21 1926 = 25/7 — Personal Year Number and Ruling Number 7
April 21 1971 = 25/7 — Personal Year Number 7
April 21 1972 = 26/8 — Personal Year Number 8
April 21 1973 = 27/9 — Personal Year Number 9
April 21 1974 = 28/10 — Personal Year Number 1
April 21 1975 = 29/11 — Personal Year Number 2
April 21 1976 = 30/3 — Personal Year Number 3
April 21 1977 = 31/4 — Personal Year Number 4
April 21 1978 = 32/5 — Personal Year Number 5
April 21 1979 = 33/6 — Personal Year Number 6
April 21 1980 = 25/7 — Personal Year Number 7

It can be readily seen that the years of the 1970s decade, and the first of the 1980s reveal a smooth continuity of numerological change to create the flowing cycle of Personal Year Numbers. This cycle will be found to have its flood (as Shakespeare so capably expressed it) and its drought, with intermediate stabilising periods.

These Personal Year Numbers move in cycles from 1 to 9, then back to 1, repeating for as long as the person is on earth. Unlike the Ruling Numbers, we do not use the 10, 11 or 22/4 as Personal Year Numbers, for they do not represent special influence. Rather, they tend to create confusion for the student in grasping the essence and smooth flow of cyclic changes over the nine personal years.

Personal Year 1   This is the most powerful year for adjustment, as would be expected after the previous dynamic year of change (9). This vibration encourages us to develop confidence in the power of noble convictions, to dare to be different and become a little freer of the limitations society tends to impose upon thinking people. It is an excellent time to break with old habits. Adaptation to an improved lifestyle often demands such a break. It is an especially powerful year for improving ourselves financially and for buying and selling on a wide scale, such as with real estate, business interests or investments. However, the most significant and permanent successes will only be achieved when people's motives are genuinely for the common good, free of materialistic self-seeking or any similarly unworthy attitude. When people are on the Path, living a purposeful life, this is a year of exciting long-term progress resulting from individual effort.

Ruling 10 people will find adaptation so effortless this year that they can easily be lulled into an attitude of frivolity. They must be careful to avoid recklessness, especially in financial matters, and take heed not to succumb to egocentricity. With self-discipline, they will find it a year of significant material growth.

Personal Year 2   Spiritual development is the feature of this year. It is not a year for major change, but rather one in which the cultivation of improved spiritual awareness is undertaken with success. The practice of meditation is especially beneficial this year for it is a period in which personal evaluation should take place, a year to take firm control of the emotions in order to discriminate between actions and reactions. After the progress which usually attends the previous two years there is a tendency to rest on one's laurels or lapse into complacency. It is then that negativeness has its opportunity to develop the reactive conditions of fear and nervousness. Emotional upsets are not uncommon consequences of such sensitivity. However, they should not be regarded as a natural part of this year — rather are they unnatural, for they indicate that one has temporarily lost control. Hence the importance of maintaining command of one's sensitivities, employing them actively as guides to constructive living and being especially responsive to their guidance during this Personal Year 2. Under this vibration physical effort depends greatly on spiritual awareness.

Ruling 2 and ruling 11 people will, during this year, find an increased level of psychic awareness as the emphasis shifts from the physical and material to the spiritual. Their co-operation with this development by allowing time for meditation and spiritual studies will considerably improve their confidence through a higher understanding of life, especially if combined with the helping of others.

Personal Year 3   We now pass into a year when mental activity reaches a high point. Under this vibration our thinking and observing faculties are attuned to an acute peak of alertness. It is a year when the intellect thirsts for expression and knowledge. For some it could involve studies of an academic nature; others might prefer to investigate life and its philosophies; and others might seek enlightenment through personal involvement. The usual means of mental expansion in this year are either by the commencement of an educational course or by extensive travel. Both would be beneficial, the choice being determined by people's Ruling Number, age, environment and personal requirements. March is the best month for the start of such activities and June the next most powerful. It is unusual for a major change to occur during this year, although the influence of the peaks of Pyramids of Maturity (see Stage 10) can rule otherwise. On the lighter side of the Personal Year 3 we should recognise the need for balance by ensuring that time is allowed for humour and happy occasions; bright friendships are of primary importance. Towards the end of this year, especially after September, care should be taken to obtain plenty of rest to ensure the body's nerve energy supply is maintained at a high level. This enables us to more capably handle the trials of the year to come.

Ruling 3 people must control the high level of mental alertness prevailing this year and direct their thinking along new or advanced educational paths. If they fail to do so they could become destructively critical of almost everyone and everything around them. This will neither improve their popularity nor their state of happiness. In studies they make exceptional progress during this year provided they do not succumb to distractions.

Personal Year 4   Physical influences are the most prevalent under this vibration. It must be recognised as a year of consolidation, vital to the state of people's health. Following the last few years of progressive change, we must now allow the body to catch up, to rest and recharge its nervous system. Characterised by the figure of the square, symbolising the 4, this is a year when a feeling of confinement prevails, indicating that the contemplation of change could be unwise. Those who do not follow the need for treading water, allowing time for relaxation and adjustment, could find themselves in a state of disharmony, leading to frustration, confusion and fear. Any attempt at major changes in our affairs or lifestyle during this year are rarely successful, leading instead to material losses in either finances or health, or both. Only adequate rest and relaxation will ensure that our nervous energy is not depleted to a point of chronic enervation. People who are normally regarded as highly strung, whose nerves are ever tense and whose sensitivity is naturally acute, should be especially careful to avoid any disharmonies in their dealings with others. A relaxed vacation during this year is most beneficial. No new financial ventures should be contemplated or commenced by anyone in their Personal Year 4, nor should any major change be undertaken in vocation or place of abode. This situation will ease after the month of August, but only if the need for ample relaxation and time for adjustment during the year has been respected; otherwise, the nerves could suffer well into the following year.

Ruling 4 people cannot be blamed for feeling very frustrated under the personal 4 vibration. Invariably they will fail to recognise it as a year of consolidation, trying instead to perpetuate the progress achieved during the previous few years. As a result their nerves take a severe battering. They must be prepared to increase their rest period in bed each night and avoid too many nerve-depleting experiences such as TV thrillers. The inclusion in their diet of adequate B-complex vitamin-rich natural foods (such as wheatgerm, yeast, raw seeds and nuts), or B-complex vitamin tablets (a less desirable alternative) is of considerable benefit to restoring nerve energy. Ruling 22/4 people should accept the same advice, but with the additional suggestion that they recognise their more spiritual essence and organise their daily routines to permit periods for meditation and relaxation in silence. They must assiduously avoid personal conflicts for the sake of health and nerves, concentrating their attention on organisational activities at which they easily excel.

Personal Year 5

Again, this is no year for material progress or for major changes in people's financial positions. But it is a year of strengthened psychic abilities, especially the control of emotions and the conservation of nervous energy. Heightened awareness in spiritual and compassionate matters can mark this year as one of artistic progress. Indeed, it is an excellent opportunity to engage in the development of artistic talents or to embrace studies of a spiritual nature. Although generally not a year for major change, it is nonetheless one in which a decision is often taken to move out of the city and away to the country. So long as it does not involve a huge financial outlay or commitment beyond that already existing, such a move would generally be highly successful, especially during the months of May through October. Whenever possible, the peace of the countryside should be enjoyed during this year to harmonise and nourish the nerves and to calm our spirits in the atmosphere of tranquility and freedom.

Ruling 5 people will find this a year in which their desires for freedom become noticeably stronger. However, they must realise that it is not always physical freedom they need, although it is sometimes easy to believe it to be so. Their primary need is for freedom of expression. This can best be achieved through the arts. Singing, playing a musical instrument, painting, making pottery or any similar form of artistic expression provides excellent release for the nerves, helping these individuals attain an all-important personal calmness.

Personal Year 6

This is a year for creative development. New projects undertaken during this period of creative value and for the common good will succeed. It is an especially successful year for the formation of public-spirited corporations and important business associations. Under the vibration of the 6 considerable personal emphasis is directed towards the home and the loved ones. It is often a year when deep friendships are made or cemented into marriage and when the home features prominently. It is also a very conducive vibration under which to develop our creative faculties. If people are living negatively this can be a most difficult year. Their emphasis on the home can become one of intense anxiety, leading at times to arguments and broken homes. Yet when living simply and constructively we can make this year one of beauty and creative achievement.

Ruling 6 people could find this a very difficult year to handle unless they are absorbed in a suitable creative activity. When so engaged their natural abilities will be strengthened in the course of the year. It then becomes a very progressive year. But those who worry or become overanxious, especially with regard to the home, will find this a very burdensome year which severely drains their nerves and their patience. When this occurs they must realise that balanced creative expression has been missing from their lives and that efforts to remedy this omission will significantly improve their emotional state.

Personal Year 7

Similar to the Personal Year 4, this is one of consolidation when no major progress should be expected. It is a year of learning, as can only occur through personal experience. For many this means sacrifice. When we fail to accept the guidance of the higher powers and, instead, live reactively and thoughtlessly, we expose ourselves to the need for firm corrective measures — prompt karma, we might call it. Such sacrifices invariably mean losses in material effects, in love, or in health. But these all have purpose, for they are designed to awaken us and return us to our Path so that we may improve our understanding of life. It is especially important to avoid any large scale business dealings or financial investments during this year. Realise that this is a year of consolidation, of placing in perspective the experiences of recent years to prepare for the forthcoming cyclic peak under the next Personal Years 9 and 1.

Ruling 7 people will often suffer seemingly severe hardships under this vibration. But their experiences will invariably appear far worse to the outsider. These people are not unfamiliar with sacrifice, as this is their established pattern of learning; and will be until they attain a significant measure of awareness. Once this is achieved, they become excellent teachers and helpers to mankind, thereby fulfilling the purpose intended of their Ruling Number.

Personal Year 8   During this year we emerge from the consolidating trough of our nine-year cycle on the rising wave of growth and prosperity as it approaches the next peak. Many new opportunities appear under this vibration, although it is often well into the second half of the year before they are recognised and not until the following year that they reach their zenith. The lessons of the previous four years have done much to prepare for the independence which this year has to offer us. For some it will be in the form of a significant improvement in financial affairs, especially likely during the period from August to December; for the majority, there will emerge a spiritual independence whereby they recognise how much emotional control and understanding of life they have achieved and how much more emphasis they now place on living (acting), rather than existing (reacting).

Ruling 8 people already have an appreciable measure of independence. When compounded by the vibrations of this Personal Year, they may become aloof, often finding it difficult to communicate fluently with those near and dear to them, whom they often take for granted. They must learn to be more expressive, for in so doing they will achieve a measure of happiness they had not previously known. Such sharing will not minimise their independence; it will help others to understand it.

Personal Year 9   The Personal Year 9 is always found at the crest of a cycle. It is very much a year of change, although the changes are sometimes not fully recognised during that year. They can be of such nature as to delay physical manifestation until the following year. These changes will vary considerably over the lifetime of each person, becoming especially pronounced during the twenty-seven-year duration of people's Pyramids. This important year is usually highly suited to travel, long journeys being the most successful if commenced or planned in March, June or September. It is also a year for the making of new and exciting friendships and the termination of those older friendships which have been outgrown. Further, it is a year for the squaring of debts and for extending forgiveness to anyone with whom you are at variance. A strong sense of humanitarian responsibility, tolerance and improved understanding will noticeably prevail during this year.

Ruling 9 people will be under no doubt as to the importance of this year for they will feel its vibrant power in their every action. It should be their year of most notable success. For them it is clearly the crest of a cycle and of increased responsibility in whatever humanitarian field they express themselves. For those with intense ambition, special care should be taken that they do not allow their enthusiasm to become overly demanding. Remember, all ambition must be tempered with wisdom — just as a fire must be contained for beneficent warmth, for if unrestrained it causes destruction.

STAGE 10
The Pyramids—Your Years of Maturity

Ancient Egyptian priests knew it. Greeks of the Golden Age following the Pythagorean methods were taught it. The early Christian' fathers recognised it. But modern man is only slowly discovering it — that his maximum potential of physical, mental and spiritual fulfilment can only occur when he matures to a point of, as Pythagoras so succinctly expressed it, 'acquiring empire over the self'. This is the goal of life's middle or mature phase, that vital period of growth now symbolised by a group of four Pyramids.

So important is this second phase of life, the period of real maturity, that the ancients related it symbolically to their inimitable Pyramids. In our study of human life through numerology we follow the same tradition and represent this period in Pyramid form.

To the ancients, Pyramids had profound significance. Symbolically they represented man's aspirations towards his creator and perfection; materially they were so constructed as to attract and concentrate great power, as well as to perpetuate the secrets of eternal life. The total construction was not meant to be merely an impressive funereal edifice. It was instead a gigantic power source within which the knowledge and wisdom of the buried leaders could be amplified and then spiritually broadcast throughout the nation, thereby perpetuating their omniscient influence over the affairs of the people. Today, it is as though the ancient power of the Pyramids is available to man in his living state of awareness. He does not need a post-mortem structure to amplify his power. He can knowingly achieve this as he reaches maturity in earthly life.

A special concentration of powers develops in human life once adolescence concludes, when one's affairs become one's own responsibility. It is then also that people's influence over the affairs of others commences to gain strength. This is the period of maturity, when the seeds of further karmic development are sown.

Provided neither karmic nor environmental influences decree otherwise, human life expectancy encompasses three phases of unfoldment: adolescence, maturity and fulfilment. The initial period, adolescence, prevails from birth, through the many changes in bodily development, until physical maturity is reached. At a predetermined age it gives way to the development of mental maturity. This continues for a period of twenty-seven years, by which time people reach a level of fulfilment in proportion to the success thus far achieved. The degree of maturity attained prepares them for spiritual development during the third phase of life. Such is the three-fold progression of natural earthly life.

To students of metaphysics it is no secret that certain karmic obligations can be so demanding during the early years of a human life that the life might be terminated prior to reaching its real maturity. If this is the plan for a life its purpose is comparatively simple and is fulfilled early. But such destinies have always been in a minority and are becoming even rarer as karmic progress becomes swifter (see Stage 14). With average human life expectancy now around its highest in the history of this planet, we can usually look to our life developing beyond its adolescent years through maturity and well into the years of fulfilment. As a consequence, each time souls now incarnate, their potential for higher evolution is markedly increased.

During the period of adolescence human lives are primarily concerned with physical experience. Even though their cycles of change, as revealed by the Personal Year Numbers, indicate varying degrees of influence of a mental or spiritual nature, the overriding emphasis is essentially physical. Basically, it is by the five physical senses that juveniles confront earthly life, are disciplined, recognise their relationship to parents and environment, then commence to gain some insight into the existence of their individuality. Throughout their years of scholastic involvement, young humans undergo such marked changes in physical development that their whole existence is focused on physical expression — their own, as well as that of others. The deceleration of physical growth in the latter teenage years is usually succeeded by accelerated mental and emotional activity. This is a period of many hurts and many triumphs, but it brings people to the threshold of real maturity when the physical playground is no longer the sole centre of attraction.

Essentially a period of mental activity, the development of real maturity is directed towards emotional control and the acquiring of enlightenment and wisdom. Strong cyclic influences of varying physical and spiritual activity will continue to prevail during this period, while the in-dwelling individuality emerges and the Inner Self is discovered. The level of success we achieve during our years of maturity will generally determine the degree of fulfilment we may realise during our third phase of life. No major change in lifestyle can be made in these last years with the same measure of success as during the years of maturity.

As the world proceeds toward the closing years of this twentieth century, the increasing complexities imposed upon human life make the need for a clearer understanding of its purpose all the more essential. This is especially important if we are to achieve the full potential of maturity.

Numerological analysis reveals to us that the period of maturity is of twenty-seven years' duration. It commences at different ages for people with different Pathways, as indicated by their Ruling Number, varying between twenty-five and thirty-four years. We symbolise this period on a diagram of pyramids and, for this reason, call it the period of the Pyramids. The twenty-seven years of the Pyramids comprise three nine-year cycles. The age at which they commence for each person is found by deducting their Ruling Number from the number 36. Reasons for the use of 36 have their origin, so far as we now know, back in Egyptian times (probably even back to the Atlantean era). It was a number of important esoteric significance in the building of the Pyramids of Egypt, an importance which carries through into practical terms when we see how it ensures that all people commence life on the pyramids at a peak year, a Personal Year 9 (which is 36 reduced to a single digit, $3 + 6$).

Before we look at the ages at which people of different Ruling Numbers attain their Pyramid Peaks, we should investigate the numerological foundations for the construction of our Pyramids. These foundations consist of three separate numbers, each derived from the date of birth. They are the numbers of the month, the day and the year (in that order), each reduced to its single digit.

CONSTRUCTION OF YOUR PYRAMIDS

The most unambiguous manner of describing the construction of the Pyramids for analysing progress during the years of maturity is best achieved by example. For this purpose we shall use the birthdate of Queen Elizabeth II — April 21, 1926.

Step 1   Reduce birthdate to single digits, ensuring that the month number is written before that of the day, thus April is translated to 4, the 21st day to 3, with the year 1926 adding to 18 and reducing to 9:

$$4 \; - \; 3 \; - \; 9$$

Step 2   Build the first Pyramid on the first two numbers:

The Peak Number for this Pyramid is obtained by adding together the two numbers at the base of the Pyramid and, if necessary, this would be resolved to a single digit. But in this example it is already a single digit — 7 is therefore placed inside the first Peak unchanged. (If the base numbers were 7 and 8, the Peak Number would be 6, the total of 7 and 8 resolved to a single digit.)

Step 3 Build the second Pyramid on the second and third base numbers:

The Peak Number for this second Pyramid is obtained by adding 3 and 9, the numbers at the base. These total 12, which has to be resolved to a single digit by adding 1 and 2. Thus, the Peak Number for the second Pyramid is 3.

Step 4 Build the third Pyramid on the two existing Pyramids:

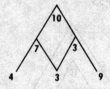

The Peak Number for the third Pyramid is the total of the first and second Peak Numbers. This is also resolved to a single digit, except if the total is 10 or 11 in which instances it remains as these full numbers. Our example shows that the Queen's third Peak Number is 10.

Step 5 The final Pyramid is built around the other three because

109

its base numbers are the first and third — 4 and 9 in this example:

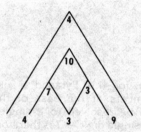

The Peak Number for this fourth Pyramid is the total of its two base numbers, 4 and 9, being 13. As with the other Peaks, this is resolved to a single digit, resulting in a Peak Number of 4; but if the total were 10 or 11 they would not be reduced. It is important to note that these two double numbers are only used if they appear on the third or fourth Peaks, for here their stronger spiritual influence achieves special importance only as the third phase of life is approached.

Step 6   We now have four Pyramids, diagramatically representing the Queen's current stage of life. The Peak of each Pyramid indicates very important years in the period of the Queen's maturity. The age at which she reaches the first Peak is the chronological age of commencement of her maturity. This is found by deducting her Ruling Number, 7, from 36. Thus the age of 29 is placed adjacent to the first peak, together with the year at which this age is reached, viz. 1955.

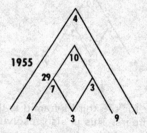

Step 7   The ages attained at the remaining Pyramid peaks ad-

vance in nine-year intervals. Thus, the second peak is reached at age 38 in the year 1964; the third peak at age 47 in 1973; the fourth peak at age 56 in 1982. When these numbers are placed on the Pyramid diagram, it is completed thus:

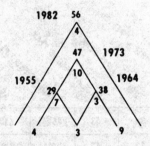

As an exercise to ensure you completely understand this important method, take a large piece of paper and write on it the birthdate of Prince Philip — June 10, 1921. Now close the book and set up the diagram of his Pyramids; then check to see how much you have learned.

Here is the complete Birthchart and the Pyramids for Prince Philip:

$$6 - 10 - 1921 = 20/2$$

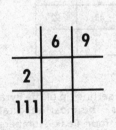

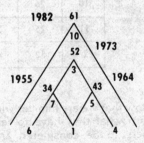

If your effort did not result in an identical diagram, it is suggested that you recheck your methods step by step. It is important that these methods be thoroughly understood before further progress can be made.

We must also be certain of the year of commencement on the Pyramids and the ages at which people of each Ruling Number arrive at their Peaks. The following chart will be of material assistance to those who do not wish to do their own calculation:

RULING NUMBER OF PERSON	AGE AT FIRST PEAK	AGE AT SECOND PEAK	AGE AT THIRD PEAK	AGE AT FOURTH PEAK
2	34	43	52	61
3	33	42	51	60
4	32	41	50	59
5	31	40	49	58
6	30	39	48	57
7	29	38	47	56
8	28	37	46	55
9	27	36	45	54
10	26	35	44	53
11	25	34	43	52
22/4	32	41	50	59

Now that we are familiar with the setting up of the Pyramids, let us learn what they have to teach us. The most important set of numbers to be considered are the four Peak Numbers on the Pyramids.

THE PEAK NUMBERS

Due to the contrasting conditions necessary for each of us to achieve a well-balanced maturity, we need additional help to that normally available from the Ruling Number. We get our supplementary support from those four Peak Numbers on our Pyramids. The object of the Peak Numbers is to provide a valuable source of additional thrust at specific periods during the maturing years. For all who have karmically evolved beyond the barbarian stage (as has every thinking person), these numbers exert a special influence which commences towards the end of the year prior to the Peak year (Personal Year 8), and rises to its acme of strength during the Peak year (Personal Year 9). This influence can be sustained for up to four years, significantly diminishing towards the close of the Personal Year 3 following the Peak year.

Peak Number 1 will only be found on either (occasionally on both) the first or the second Pyramids. On the third or fourth Pyramids, it becomes a 10. The 1 is an intensely practical number, indicating that a period of individual effort is about to prevail, a period of definite personal expression. For most it will mean separation from previous involvements in which some degree of disharmony was inhibiting personal development, such as in marriage, business associations or social intercourse. You may be assured that no marriage, business relationship or friendship will be severed unless it had already served its purpose. Some people will choose to avoid such separations with all possible effort, preferring to maintain the status quo. Notwithstanding, they will doubtless recognise a change in the nature of the relationship because they begin to exert more of their own individuality and become more expressive. The more spiritually advanced they are (in other words, the older the soul), the more they will exert their individuality this year and henceforth. The direction of their activities is usually consistent with their Ruling Number; the manner in which they express will depend on their personality strengths indicated by their Birthchart.

Peak Number 2 introduces a period when stronger spiritual values emerge. Life-style and habits will subtly embrace either a more intuitive or a more emotional manner. Whether the spiritual emphasis manifests as an improved state of awareness (its positive, most constructive form), or as a state of heightened emotions (its reactive and defeating form), will depend on the level of maturity thus far achieved. Obviously intuitive ability cannot be expected to develop if the individual is held captive by emotion. This is usually a period of hard work and slow progress in material affairs, but we cannot have it both ways. Remember, there is a right time for everything and one of the most important applications of this science of numbers is to learn what our needs are and the right way, as well as the right time, to deal with them. To enforce material progress when under the influence of the Peak Number 2 would be to invite frustrations, conflicts and emotional enervation.

Peak Number 3   is always a period when the emphasis should be directed towards the intellectual. It is an important period of learning, of reviewing and of analysing. Many people find the urge for travel particularly accentuated under the guidance of this vibration. At this period in their lives travel for such people assumes a very important role as a means of learning and expanding their insight into life. If they do not allow their mental faculties scope for positive expansion, they run the risk of becoming destructively critical, exacting and, not surprisingly, quite unpopular.

Peak Number 4   brings with it increased material power. This might be expressed in any number of ways, depending upon the general level of maturity, Ruling Number and Birthchart characteristics. For those people who are prepared for hard work, much can be achieved under this vibration. For those who need to acquire additional knowledge in dealing with the faculties of sense to round off their maturity and who are prepared to involve themselves in physical work, vital development will reward their efforts. But those who become overly ambitious, mercenary or covetous will find this period one of loss, rather than gain. Even though they might work harder, they will make no discernible progress while their motives are so egocentric. This can lead to a serious strain on their nerves and general state of health which can only be corrected after they reassess their motives.

Peak Number 5   usually introduces significant changes to people's emotional state. These are created through the emergence of spiritual growth and understanding which leads to greater personal freedom. It is a period through which the psychic powers undergo considerable strengthening, thereby facilitating an improved level of emotional control. In turn this reduces reactiveness to people and to situations. As a consequence a greater measure of personal liberty develops which prepares the way for increased spiritual awareness. Those who in earlier years were anxious about their financial security now have the means for dispelling such worries with a more balanced view of their real needs and environmental influences.

Peak Number 6   brings with it a very strong power for creative development. It is a period when the highest spiritual and mental faculties can combine to reveal to man his vital role in the limitless plan of creation. Such sublime awareness will rarely become apparent to any but the more mature, more highly evolved people. For the majority, those who identify with physical possessiveness, this becomes a period of intense home involvement

114

or, if unmarried, a hankering for settling down in their own home. Tendencies to worry about the home or to rush into marriage should be recognised as merely the procreative counterparts of what would otherwise be a powerful creative drive. Wisdom and patience should be exercised to avoid the need for the hurtful lessons which are attracted when emotions dominate people's affairs.

Peak Number 7 can bring many surprising changes into people's lives. It is the period when we are called upon to share all we have learned thus far. By so doing we experience tremendous progress in our own unfolding, for there is no better system of learning than that of teaching. This is an intensely empirical period in life, for it requires us to undergo much testing. If successful we qualify for the higher teachings which await us during this year; if we have not yet matured to a point of acceptable growth, we must spend more time in preparatory development. Most people during this period of vibrationary influence are called upon to undertake some form of teaching, but not necessarily in conventional scholastic fields. More often their teaching is associated with post-academic fields of human evolvement such as yoga, natural therapies, spiritual awareness and artistic development.

Peak Number 8 denotes independence as the prevailing force during this very powerful period. Whether independence develops through artistic or commercial involvements will, of course, depend on the Ruling Number: if it is an even number, financial success is indicated; if an odd number, success through artistic (or for some people academic) expression is more likely. Great care must be taken that the power of this vibration is used constructively and that opposing individuals or limiting situations are not allowed to inhibit its transmission. The result of such influences will be clearly discernible in an uncharacteristic aloofness — the effort of the soul struggling to achieve independent expression.

Peak Number 9 introduces a period of pronounced humanitarian activity. This vibration brings with it special opportunities to serve mankind. It is also a period when intense mental involvement is necessary for the greatest success to be achieved — analysing and assessing the needs of others, planning for major changes in vocation, and re-evaluating long-standing relationships and environmental surroundings. Many people attempt to make demands on your time and energy during this period. Some are in genuine need and provide important opportunities to serve; some will be artificially contrived to attract your sympathy. These latter cases should be treated as individuals needing awakening. Our discriminatory and analysing abilities will certainly be tested and strengthened by such experiences. While some people under this

115

vibration will need to remain at home and be of service, others will be moved to travel to undergo important lessons in development. Everyone, during the first year of influence following the attainment of this Peak, will find important changes occurring in their lives. If not involving travel, they will almost without exception move house, change jobs or form new circles of acquaintances. Any one of a number of these alterations in lifestyle can occur, depending on the nature of the responsibilities necessary to the prevailing stage in growth toward maturity.

Peak Number 10   can only occur on the third or fourth Pyramid Peaks, as maturity approaches its zenith. It brings a special strength, a unique power for relating to the needs of others during important periods of adjustment in their lives. This ability is the happy consequence of people's own living experiences and the training instilled by them. With the emphasis on mind power, as indicated by the 9 in every birthdate this century, a considerable amount of mental adjustment is needed to remould outlooks and lifestyles as the new age approaches. Those older souls who have a Peak Number 10 during this period assume critically important roles in guiding and encouraging those in need. This is an exciting responsibility which confers upon the giver as many benefits as upon the receiver.

Peak Number 11   is the second of the two Peak Numbers which can only occur on either the third or fourth Peaks. As with the Peak Number 10, a high level of maturity is necessary to handle its power. Peak Number 11 indicates that a considerable amount of spiritual accountability is demanded. Yet the demand will never exceed the individual's capacity. It is a period of high intuitiveness, when the most inspired actions become possible. However, there are certain spiritual requirements necessary for the optimum potential of this period to be realised. These involve compassion, temperance, Integrity and the practice of meditation. Compassion means far more than its modern limited interpretation of commiseration and comfort. It is the practice of philanthropy, the sharing of love in its highest spiritual sense. In very practical terms it implies thoughtfulness for, and harmony with, all life, especially human life. Temperance is the expression of balance and moderation in all undertakings, while meditation is an exercise in enlightenment through a relaxed mind and body, restoring complete harmony to the mind, the body and the heart. While these disciplines are in practise, the virtue of impeccable integrity must prevail throughout actions and thoughts, thereby ensuring that no negative forces can impede spiritual unfoldment, the supreme purpose of this period.

The qualities of maturity developed during this twenty-seven-year period in life bring with them the mental and material independence necessary for the expansion of wisdom during the third and final period of earthly human life we call fulfilment.

THE YEARS OF FULFILMENT

This third phase of life should complete the transition from our younger worldliness to the wisdom and peace which accompany realisation. No longer should our thoughts and actions be held captive under the yokes of ambitiousness, anxiety and agitation of those earlier years as a novice. Graduation has occurred. Private and public expressions are now those of an initiate — relaxed, confident and noble.

The sixty or so years thus far accumulated in the body should have matured us to a realisation that only by the twin virtues of truth and wisdom can we now attain the fulfilment intended of our third phase of life. Our loyalties now become distinctly two-fold. Outwardly we must do everything possible to share the benefits of our own worldly experiences with the general aim of assisting the renewal of our nation's cultural heritage. Inwardly preparation must be made for the inevitable journey beyond the Earthly Plane.

With growing richness in years, senior citizens offer to the younger generations a fountain of wisdom unknown to those less mature. Of this virtue Oriental cultures are astutely conscious, evidenced by so many older people in government than we find in the Occident. The west has yet to learn that youthful vitality must be balanced by mature wisdom for lasting success in life.

STAGE 11
The Sun Signs and Their Elements

This book is not designed to teach astrology, but astrological influences play such a powerful role in understanding personality and individuality that it would be highly negligent of us not to investigate these important factors in self-analysis.

The close relationship between astrology and numerology is evident to all who have studied both sciences. They both provide an insight into life, yet we always find an explicit preference with students and counsellors for one over the other. The basis for such preference will not always be apparent, nor does the reason really matter — an academic scientist might exert a similar preference in his study of physics or chemistry, yet they are so related that he must have a sound working knowledge of both. Actually, this analogy between the two metaphysical sciences and the two physical sciences is very illustrative, for it offers many parallels to our studies here.

Numerology and astrology are the two most scientific and reliable metaphysical sciences for the investigation into the Inner Self, for the understanding of what makes up our individuality. Chemistry and physics are two of the most essential physical sciences for the study of the material universe, the understanding of the outer self. (Even applied to nutritional studies and processes of human digestion they fall within the category of the outer self, in comparison to the spiritual and mental, the essential being of man.)

As one of the metaphysical keystones, astrology is more than the mere study of heavenly bodies. It is the ancient science of the study of the heavenly bodies and their relationship to human life. Its origin far predates recorded history, lying possibly beyond the remote Atlantean period. We know that the Atlanteans used it extensively, conferring their knowledge upon their heirs on both sides of that ocean named after them. Their influence was so profound that it penetrated far beyond the shores of the Atlantic, with traces of it being extant even today in Central and South America, as well as in Lebanon, Greece, Egypt, Crete, etc.

The ancients were not scientific people, as we understand the meaning of the word today. But they did recognise the powerful influence over their affairs exerted by the sun and the moon, along with the mysterious magnetism of the planets. Not only were these influences apparent in the formation of the weather and the tides, but also in farming and, most appropriately, in human personality. Hence those early studies evolved, revealing the influences exerted by the positions of various heavenly bodies at the time of a person's birth. Those same wise ancients also observed the effect on human nature of numerical vibrations.

With the establishment of the modern scientific system by Pythagoras, those ancient observations (for even then they were ancient) were expanded and the sciences of astrology and numerology took a great leap forward.

Always, there have been people who would exploit the gullible. It is not any worse today than in earlier times. But it was the exploiters of astrology and numerology in ancient times, particularly during biblical times, who gave these sciences a spurious reputation. It must be emphasised that these disciplines are not predictive arts to be used to hold the fear of a calamitous future over those they seek to exploit, as did the astrologers of Nebuchadnezzar's court.

Of immediate concern now is to recognise that we are not dealing with quackery or the work of the devil when we discuss and employ these metaphysical sciences. Indeed, we know that from the study of the heavenly bodies and their relationship to human life (astrology) was born the academically esteemed science of astronomy. The metaphysical always predetermines the physical; everything in life testifies to this. But again we are not primarily interested in the physical — if the astronomers wish to restrict their studies to the physical aspects of the heavenly bodies, we will leave it to them. We find these studies most relevant when they relate to human life. Each of the heavenly bodies has strong peculiarities of its own. The astronomers study their physical character but we are more concerned with how their more subtle peculiarities affect us. That is what astrology teaches.

When a person is born we know that certain vibrationary influences prevail which can be analysed numerologically to reliably assess the individuality. The basis for this assessment, which has been the subject of the previous ten stages of this book, is the earthly date of birth. Now we will consider that, at the time of birth, the earth itself received unique vibratory emanations from the sun and the sun's position in relation to stellar constellations also exercised certain significant influences.

Each of the twelve astrological Sun Signs exerts an influence which lasts for a period averaging one calendar month, the twelve collectively totalling a full calendar year — one complete revolution of earth around the sun. So widely used is the science of astrology that every person knows the name of his Sun Sign, whether or not he understands what it represents in his life. The basic characteristics of each sign are given in this stage, but it must be understood that they are by no means exhaustive. The following are, instead, summaries of the most salient aspects of each sign, with special emphasis on their health factors.

Usually the twelve Sun Signs are represented in circular form, but for our purposes they are better represented in chart form:

TRIPLICITY (Lesson)	FIRE (Compassion)	EARTH (Service)	AIR (Brotherhood)	WATER (Peace)
HEAD Intellect Thought	ARIES Mar 21-Apr 20 Dynamic	TAURUS Apr 21-May 20 Steady	GEMINI May 21-Jun 20 Sensitive	CANCER Jun 21-Jul 21 Protective
MIDDLE Emotions Feeling	LEO Jul 22-Aug 22 Leadership	VIRGO Aug 23-Sep 22 Perfectionist	LIBRA Sep 23-Oct 22 Balance	SCORPIO Oct 23-Nov 22 Sex & Healing
FEET Understanding	SAGITTARIUS Nov 23-Dec 22 Gregarious	CAPRICORN Dec 23-Jan 21 Cautious	AQUARIUS Jan 22-Feb 20 Knowledge	PISCES Feb 21-Mar 20 Peacemakers

Triplicities

These are three major aspects of human expression which effectively divide the twelve signs into groups of four each. The first four signs, Aries, Taurus, Gemini and Cancer, belong to the Head Triplicity, because of their strong emphasis on mental expression. The second group of four signs, Leo, Virgo, Libra and Scorpio, belong to the Middle Triplicity, owing to the strength of their feelings and their strong emphasis on emotional expression. The third group of four signs, Sagittarius, Capricorn, Aquarius and Pisces, make up the Feet Triplicity because of their influence on insight into the origin of things and the underlying philosophy behind all creation.

It is highly beneficial to be aware of the general mode of expression preferred by people with whom we are in contact. In my practice as a counsellor and nutritionist, this has been found a consistently reliable guide to which clients and patients most easily relate: if belonging to a Head Sign, they are most receptive to reason and logic; Middle Signs are guided most by feeling and have the strongest emotions; Feet Signs seek the underlying principles, often recognising their foundation in the metaphysical domains.

The Elements
There are four basic human natures, each relating to a general purpose in life. The twelve Sun Signs are divided into these four groups. Each group contains three signs and is assigned a symbolic name of very ancient origin. These names convey essential characteristics and lessons which are common to each of the three signs, yet are expressed by them in varying manner.

Fire Signs (Aries, Leo and Sagittarius) reveal fast-moving, volatile, sometimes fiery people, with abundant nervous energy. Their major lesson in life is to understand the meaning of divine love, embracing compassion and philanthropy, by attuning to the needs of others and by giving energies in loving support for the attainment of those needs.

Earth Signs (Taurus, Virgo and Capricorn) indicate very steady and predictable people who are the most consistent and dependable friends we are likely to find. Their karmic lessons are related to being of service to their fellow man. In so being, they will elevate their consciousness beyond the earthly to the spiritual, but this is rarely achieved before the latter half of their years of maturity. Primary motivations in their earlier lives are more related to the physical world of playing, eating and doing, for it is through these involvements that they acquire the early development they need.

Air Signs (Gemini, Libra and Aquarius) are the flexible people, with quick brains and deep understanding. They are people who can often think of many different things at once, but they must take care not to allow themselves to become too involved in a wide diversity of projects, else they will tire from enervation. Brotherhood is their karmic lesson, through which they develop a deep philosophy of life by mixing with and helping people.

Water Signs (Cancer, Scorpio and Pisces) are the peaceful people — the quiet, restful ones whose presence usually brings comfort. At times, though, these people can be very emotional and lose control of their feelings. They must guard against these situations which create distress to all involved and noticeably diffuse their natural peacefulness. They have great tenacity and are exceptionally capable healers when living constructively.

The Cusps
Each of the Sun Signs discussed in the following pages and shown on the preceding chart are given dates to indicate the period of their influence. The commencing and concluding days shown for each month should be regarded as being the average of those given by a selected number of eminent astrological researchers.

Birthdates falling within a six-day period, comprising three days each side of the changeover date between any two signs, actually come within the influence of both signs. This six-day changeover period is known as the Cusp. During each Cusp period, the relationship between the joint influences of each sign is generally determined by analysing the exact position of the birthdate. For instance, the Cusp of Aries-Taurus covers the period April 18 to 23, inclusive. A person born on April 18, 19 or 20 will be influenced more by Aries, less by Taurus, but the stronger aspects of the Taurean nature will certainly prevail; anyone born on April 21, 22 or 23 will be influenced more by Taurus, less by Aries — here the stronger aspects of the Arien nature will prevail.

The Foods　　With the analysis of each of the twelve Sun Signs is offered a list of natural foods containing researched estimates of availability of the particular cell salt required. Nutrients in natural form are by far the best means for achieving dietary correction, whereas the administering of raw salts is only of value for short-term therapeutic purposes. The human body cannot easily assimilate mineral salts in their coarse form, but is designed to absorb those which nature has finely triturated through its plant kingdom. Should such foods be unavailable, or should the body be so devitalised as to demand stronger potencies, it is recommended that finely prepared biochemic cell salts in tablet or liquid form be taken for the needed recuperative period. But it must be emphasised that combining a corrected mental attitude with dietary correction is the only permanent method for maintaining health.

Due to their high level of nutritional potency, some of the foods appear in the lists of more than one sign. One cannot improve upon raw unsalted nuts and seeds, soya beans, green vegetables and many of the dried fruits and grains as sources of almost the entire range of biochemic cell salts required by the human body.

ARIES — MARCH 21 TO APRIL 20

Characteristic Expression　　Arians have very active brains, always seeking to learn things, always thinking and planning. They are high-spirited people, dynamic, volatile, courageous, witty and potentially very good scholars. Learning is important to them, as are bright social associations. They are rarely lost for words and ever ready to verbally defend themselves and their actions. For those who live constructively, responsibility is their second nature; in its expression they find guidance constantly available from their acute intuition. The other side of their nature is to be reckless, headstrong and often quite fierce — this is when they live destructively and become a liability to society. Factors which could swing the personality away from its naturally constructive expression are often traceable to a mineral deficiency in the diet, particularly of the most vital cell salt for Arians, potassium phosphate.

Negative Tendencies to be Surmounted
Due to their high level of cerebral energy Arians can be extremely impatient with others. However, with a loved one they can show so much patience as to be easily imposed upon. This will effectively reduce the reliability of their intuition and cause them to make some monumental errors of judgement. Even when living constructively they should take care not to overestimate their capabilities or to engage in repeatedly lengthy periods of mental activity without balancing periods of relaxation; such neglect will lead to enervation, headaches and recklessness. They must think well before speaking, especially if they intend to be critical, for Arians have a sharp tongue and a fiery temper when they lose self-control.

Health Aspects
Aries relates to the cerebrum, the brain of man. Hence a physical characteristic usually related to Arians is a large head. They often have a larger than average brain and require dietary emphasis which will provide extra nourishment to the brain cells and nerve fluid. The biochemic cell salt most useful in this regard is known as Kali Phos — potassium phosphate. It can be consumed in a supplementary form as a powder or liquid following Dr William Schuessler's biochemic tradition. But if while taking this supplement the Arian adheres to a conventional, high acid diet based on processed and refined foods, a high meat intake, tea, coffee and/or alcohol, his hyperacid condition will negate the alkalising benefits of the cell salt. He is far better advised to alter his diet to embrace natural foods, with special emphasis on those richest in natural potassium phosphate, as listed according to availability:

> yeast — edible brewers and torula varieties;
> soya grits and, for those seeking milk, soya milk;
> soya beans — soaked for twenty-four hours, then steamed;
> wheatgerm and wheat bran — both must be fresh and raw;
> sunflower seeds — either sprouted or as raw whole kernels;
> chickpeas (garbanzos) and lentils;
> raw, unsalted nuts — especially almonds, brazils and
> pistachios;
> rye — sprouted is best, next is freshly stoneground.

A deficiency of potassium phosphate can be generally recognised as affecting mental processes manifesting in such symptoms as migraine, extreme nervousness, frequent hysteria, mental exhaustion, psychosis, paranoia, wild fancies and forebodings, etc.

123

Karmic Lesson   Arians must learn the meaning of selfless love, recognising its marked difference to physical desire. Compassion is the highest expression of universal love, so this virtue must become a part of their every thought, word and deed. Vital to the development of compassion is the mastery of emotions, especially temper, anger and jealousy.

TAURUS — APRIL 21 TO MAY 20

Characteristic Expression   Taureans are dominating, strong and persistent people who find their easiest form of expression to be through movement. They are extremely stable and solid friends, highly reliable and predictable. They are also very orthodox, which makes them slow to accept new ideas. Taurus governs the cerebellum, the lower brain, actually the nerve centre regulating physical movement; hence the initial response from a Taurean is to do something, rather than think about it. This creates reactions, rather than actions, giving rise to emotional involvement and passionate expression. Nevertheless, this is an Earth Sign, a stabilising influence which restrains the emotions unless some extreme irritation persists. In the normal course of events these people have kindly dispositions and are slow to anger. But when ultimately aroused, they become volcanic. Once they explode it is as though they have blown off excess steam from their escape valve, allowing a return to normal action. A further influence of earth is observed in the Taurean love for comfort, for financial security and for the good things of life — especially rich food. They have to learn that rich food is rarely a good choice for the body.

Negative Tendencies to be Surmounted   Impulsive desire plays too great a part in the life of Taureans. They must learn to reason more, to think carefully before doing — then they will act, rather than react so much. Their constancy should never be allowed to become obstinacy; their kindliness should not prompt them to become over-indulgent. Obstinancy and over-indulgence are emotional reactions which are often resorted to when fear prevails — fear of change, fear of being disliked, or of being insecure. The cerebellum is often referred to as the animal brain, for it dominates the unconscious, the body's movements and its passions. Special care should be taken to avoid emotional excesses, for passion cannot hear the voice of reason.

Health Aspects   Taurus exerts strong influence on the ears, neck, throat, liver and gall bladder. People born under this sign may have large ears, a strong neck and powerful voice (many become successful wrestlers or singers). It is not uncommon for Taureans to have weight problems brought about primarily by their tendency to over-indulge in rich food and to retain excess water in the body. The biochemic cell salt, Nat Sulph — sodium sulphate — is allied with Taurus, because this is the most efficacious expeller of water. Deficiency in this salt will induce pains in the back of the head which sometimes run down the spine, affecting the liver. As this cell salt is vital to the body's elimination of excess water, its lack will cause the body to resort to the next best means: it will produce nerve and muscular spasms, thereby inducing feverishness from the violent effort to throw off excess moisture via the bloodstream through perspiration. This is also designed to effectively reduce the body's toxicity level. The alternating fever and chill as the body cleanses, then normalises itself, together with the muscular aches from the spasms, give rise to the disease which continues to baffle physicians who have given it the name influenza. Taureans in hot and humid climates, where the breath is supercharged with moisture and people drink more (which, in turn, impedes their digestion and nutrient absorption), run greater risk of moisture retention. This often produces biliousness and sometimes predisposes towards malaria. The habit of adding common salt (sodium chloride) to foods must be avoided as this chemical works against the body's efforts to eliminate excess moisture. Contrary to popular opinion, common salt does not avert dehydration or cramps — it is a mild poison, which is the reason the body works to throw it off through its pores. If you ensure that the diet comprises foods rich in natural sodium sulphate many will also be found to contain adequate natural sodium chloride to facilitate proper cellular chemical balance. The diet should also be low in saturated fatty acids and cholesterol to ease the strain on the liver, gall bladder and arteries. Some of the most desirable foods include abundant fresh salad vegetables, particularly celery and carrots. Dried fruits such as figs, raisins and sultanas are also exceptionally nourishing to Taureans. One meal a day of fresh fruits, eaten raw, is definitely beneficial, particularly as the first meal of the day.

Karmic Lesson To recognise the difference between imprudent emotional reactions and balanced rational actions provides one of the most vital experiences in the life of a person born under the sign of Taurus. It is through service to mankind that they will learn to acquire mastery over their desires and emotions. Consequently, they will always be led into activities from which such experiences are best obtained.

GEMINI — MAY 21 TO JUNE 20

Characteristic Expression Here we are obliged to consider two people in one. Symbolically represented by the twins, the Sign of Gemini implies two personalities: one relates to the innate individuality; the other relates to the personality of social intercourse. Belonging to the Air Sign of the Head Triplicity, Gemini people are extremely sensitive and subject to rapid change of thought without warning. Their fast-moving brains tend to give them a mercurial nature, but this also implies some very beneficial abilities; viz. a reliable sense of discrimination and a gift of communication. To be instantly able to discriminate between sense and nonsense, between truth and falsehood, reality and unreality, is characteristic of Geminis. So, too, is their ability to communicate their ideas in writing, for in this way they convey their thoughts more freely than they can usually do verbally.

Negative Tendencies to be Surmounted The twin personalities of the Gemini have the disadvantage of confusing people, and even Geminis themselves can be uncertain of how to react to different situations. In general, they tend to oscillate between their lower and higher selves, their emotional and spiritual natures. Once they learn not to react, but to thoughtfully consider first, they will not be so drawn to the emotional. Until then they will find their power of concentration diminishing, with a corresponding increase in uncertainty and nervousness. Rest and relaxation are prime requisites in helping to keep their nerves under control. They should become involved in the arts, singing or playing an instrument, painting or pottery making, etc. This will provide balance to their activities and an excellent balm for their nervous systems.

Health Aspects Usually the most noticeable features of Gemini bodies are their strong shoulders, arms and hands. Their major weakness lies in their respiratory passages, with congestion a common problem. The most important of the twelve biochemic cell salts for the Gemini is Kali Mur — potassium chloride. This is both an essential blood nourisher and a vital nutrient for the proper formation of fibrin, the elastic fibrous protein which controls the formation of the skin and hair. A deficiency of potassium chloride causes thickening of fibrin, menstrual irregularities, and/or congestion when located in the respiratory passages. This might manifest as pleurisy, catarrh, pneumonia, diphtheria or bronchitis. If the congested fibrin is not thrown out of the bloodstream it can create embolisms which might clog the auricles and ventricles of the heart, ultimately resulting in its stoppage. The most satisfactory manner by which to obtain adequate potassium chloride is through the diet. Foods richest in natural potassium chloride are listed below, according to concentration of this mineral:

kelp — powder and granules;
yeast — brewers and torula;
avocados;
coconut meat — fresh;
dried fruits;
most fresh vegetables, especially asparagus, cabbage, carrot, celery, eggplant, kohlrabi, lettuce, parsnip and tomato.

Karmic Lesson   All people born under the Air Signs are motivated by a yearning for brotherhood, yet this is less obvious in the expression of the Gemini than in the Libran or Aquarian. The strong mentality of the Gemini, especially evident in their analytical approach to life and to people, is inclined to make them appear more egocentric than they are in reality. This is further aggravated by the difficulty in verbal expression which is so often a part of the Gemini nature. Deep within, Geminis know that they often misrepresent themselves. Although this is not intentional, they do not know how to correct it. They will gain release from this quandary when they acknowledge the yearning in the depths of their souls for love, companionship and understanding — in a word, brotherhood. As Geminis mature, they become more aware of the finer feelings of others, they relax more and allow the beauty of their higher selves to have greater influence over them. Usually around the third Peak of their Pyramids they become more aware of the importance of compassion and their relationship with other people.

CANCER — June 21 to July 21

Characteristic Expression   The astrological term Cancer derives from the Latin for crab and has no relationship to the malignant disease. The disease was so-called because of its tumorous nature and unrestrained reproductive ability. Symbolically, the crab tells us much about the motivation and expression of people born under this sign. They are persistent, cautious and prudent, with a deeply sensitive and tender nature. Their perseverance is enforced by a cultivated hardness which is their acquired protection for sensitive feelings. They are homeloving, with a deep concern for their castle and for the wellbeing of all within it. Their love for children is often satisfied by producing large families, for which their robust reproductive organs stand them in good stead. A further crab-like expression is the fondness these people have of collecting things for which they have no immediate use or prospect of use. Especially pronounced is the protectiveness and tenacity of those born under the Sign of Cancer. These traits underlie so much of their endeavour — physical, emotional and mental. They possess naturally good memories and strive to retain this important attribute (memory being tenacity of thought). Cancerians are often drawn to health-related fields, for they are natural healers with a deep concern for human welfare.

Negative Tendencies to be Surmounted

The acute sensitivity of Cancerians must be recognised as vital to their spiritual growth and to their loving solicitude for others. But unless they have achieved a reasonable level of self-mastery, these people risk the decline of their powers by becoming victims of their own emotions. These are manifested by nervous outbursts and moodiness, creating considerable drains on their energy reserves. Parents must be especially careful to train their Cancerian children to gain confidence in themselves and their feelings and not to react emotionally to apparent thoughtlessness demonstrated by less sensitive people. Unless they are carefully trained in self-discipline, these children could become reclusive and very shy, especially if they have the Arrow of Hypersensitivity (see page 78). In practice I have found many people who believe they are suffering from hypoglycemia are, in reality, suffering acute enervation induced by lack of control of their extreme sensitivity and by worry. This applies particularly to people born under the Sign of Cancer. They are inclined to worry about things of a domestic nature, especially the home and the welfare of their children when away from home. Fear of financial insecurity is also a great source of worry for many Cancerians. Unless these anxieties and torments are controlled, mental unbalance could follow.

Health Aspects

The Sign of Cancer exerts its major influence in the chest, spleen, solar plexis and stomach. People with this Sun Sign must be very careful with their diet because they do not have strong stomachs and easily succumb to gastric problems. When associated with worry this gives a fine prescription for ulcers. Simple, natural foods should comprise their basic diet because Cancerians must assiduously avoid highly seasoned or highly preserved foods, such as curries, peppers, pickles, strong cheeses, heavily-spiced continental-type foods, etc. The most vital biochemic cell salt for Cancerians is calcium fluoride, the cell salt which plays an essential role in the development and maintenance of the brain membranes, as well as the eyes, teeth, bones and internal cellular structure of the skin. A deficiency of this mineral salt will result from a diet lacking green vegetables, carrots, unsalted raw nuts or mild cheeses (especially cottage). These foods are excellent sources of natural calcium fluoride*. Such deficiencies can result in rough, cracked skin (loss of cellular elasticity), especially between the toes or fingers, around the anus or the mouth; early loss of memory and/or the development of an anxiety complex; cataracts in the eyes; for women, very painful periods and, ultimately, weakened reproductive organs.

Karmic Lesson   By using the mind to attain emotional control, and by conserving nervous energy, we achieve the most precious of all possessions — inner peace. Such is the essential lesson to be pursued by Cancerians. Self-control is not always easily achieved, but then, neither is anything of lasting value attained without effort. As soon as they learn to channel their sensitivities into avenues of healing and human welfare, Cancerians will have made significant progress in acquiring this harmonising peace.

LEO — JULY 22 TO AUGUST 22

Characteristic Expression   Leos are natural leaders and as alert (sometimes as aggressive) as the lion by which they are symbolised. They have considerable confidence in their own abilities and are unhappy working under authority. They are affectionate and possess enormous reserves of energy, which gives them exceptional drive and intrepid expression. Leos can also be of two extremely different natures — creative or destructive. By experience we find that the majority of them are emotional, reactive, desire-motivated people, with a reputation for instability and volatility. The more enlightened Leos are as yet in the minority, although growing awareness among new age people is swinging the pendulum. When they discover the secrets of self-control, Leo people are able to exercise their extremely powerful will for the common good and to express themselves creatively as enlightened examples of divine power in human action. They have a naturally deep sympathy for the less fortunate or those in trouble — not unexpected from people with such acute sensitivity.

Negative Tendencies to be Surmounted   Care must always be exercised in the handling of powerful sources of energy,

---

*It is especially important to understand that calcium fluoride is not the fluoride related to drinking water or tooth paste. That is sodium fluoride, a corrosive poison, classified as toxic to the body if ingested or inhaled (refer to The Merck Index of 1977 and Hawley's Chemical Dictionary, also of 1977). Sodium fluoride is largely insoluble and not found in man's natural foods, but is obtained from bauxite and fertiliser rock. Calcium fluoride is a soluble mineral salt present in small quantities in many natural foods.

129

particularly fiery human energy. With their exceptional drive Leos are inclined to overtax their heart and nerves unless they learn to practice meditation or, at the least, to incorporate periods of relaxation into their daily routines. They must expressly avoid arguments and disruptive emotional involvements such as sordid love affairs and any similar philandering for these will heavily tax their emotions, considerably depleting nervous energy. While they avidly enjoy emotional expression, Leo people must exercise moderation to ensure they do not lose control of their feelings. They are inclined to anger easily, but this will only further deplete their nervous energy. Anger places enormous strain on the muscles of the heart, far more than most people realise. Care must be taken that their natural sympathy is not imposed upon by thoughtless people, for if their sympathy is exploited it can cause such sensitive beings to feel very let down, even bitter.

Health Aspects
The heart, motor nerves (which regulate movement) and the blood are intimately related and are the most vulnerable components of Leo bodies. Thus, they must ensure that their diet is regulated to avoid too many acid-forming foods or substances such as tea, coffee, excessive protein-rich foods, chocolate, sweets, alcohol, white flour products, etc. In view of their emotional tendencies which strain the nerves and the heart, it is not surprising that Leos often suffer from a deficiency of the mineral cell salt Mag Phos — magnesium phosphate. This is the important nutrient involved in regulating nerve and muscle impulses, especially those which govern the function of the heart. There is a tendency for anyone suffering from an insufficiency of magnesium phosphate to experience spells of crying, laughter, coughing, sneezing, hiccoughs, cramps or to become quite reckless in manner. These symptoms are highly enervating but will be greatly relieved by the therapeutic application of a few grams of Mag Phos in a glass of hot water. Many sufferers from angina pectoris and mild heart spasms can overcome these acute discomforts by achieving better emotional control and by the addition to their diet of foods known to be natural sources of magnesium phosphate, particularly the following, listed in order of richness:

wheatgerm and bran;
raw, unsalted nuts and seeds;
yeast, brewers and torula;
soya beans, soya milk and soya grits;
wholewheat and rye — as cereals or in wholegrain bread;
rolled oats;
millet and buckwheat;
brown lentils — especially nourishing when sprouted and eaten raw;
blackstrap molasses.

Karmic Lesson   Every person born under the Sign of Leo is aware of his strong inner drive. Those who have not learned to channel this tremendous energy are often impatient and difficult to live with due to their frequent emotional eruptions. Life is the tamer of the lion, taking the wild animal nature and gently transforming it until it becomes a moderated, harnessed force, willing and able to be directed by the supreme intelligence. Then will the lion allow divine order to be established in all his affairs. Deep within, they are warm and compassionate people, but many Leos are not ready to exhibit this beautiful side of their nature until they reach the third phase of life (fulfilment). Life will be much more rewarding for them and for those with whom they associate when they learn to be more compassionate in their earlier years. This is the Leo's major lesson in life.

VIRGO — AUGUST 23 TO SEPTEMBER 22

Characteristic Expression   The symbol of Virgo is the virgin, meaning pure, perfect and impeccable. This accurately relates to both the nature and the body of those whose Sun Sign is Virgo. They are perfectionists, with an all-consuming concern in matters of health, yet with bodies which often experience elimination problems. In their search for perfection, Virgo people are discriminatory and analytical, demanding accuracy and detail. They never cease striving for these qualities. Virgos make firm friends, often seeking to help others improve their own lives. At times this makes them appear critical, but rarely is there anything of a condemnatory nature in their criticisms. As a rule they are more critical of themselves than of others, for they recognise that perfection must develop from within. Virgos have a natural ability for healing, but must guard against becoming overanxious about their own health. Such anxiety can give rise to an hypochondriacal tendency, with its resultant morbidity and mild depression. This negates the natural healing ability of their bodies, defeating their aim of improving the quality of life for all.

Negative Tendencies to be Surmounted   The tendency towards overanxiety is very prevalent with Virgo people, yet they rarely have any real cause for worry. A similar response is also found in their work lives where, if compelled to accept considerable responsibility, they become apprehensive of their ability. This has the effect of undermining their self-confidence. Virgos work best under encouraging, appreciative direction — and they actively seek to become involved in work. But their straining after perfection can become quite obsessive, that is until they sensibly relate it to practicalities. Virgos must guard against becoming emotional as a result of frustrations, for indeed they will experience many frustrations until the essence of matter of fact moderation is learned. Some younger souls will be tempted to seek gratification through the sexual organs, excusing this desire for sensation as their right to love. Such justifications might temporarily satisfy their ego, but their real motives never escape the Akashic Records, that total karmic history of experiences transmitted through the higher self.

Health Aspects

Some schools of astrology relate the procreative organs to Virgo but this can be misleading. Such a relationship only exists when Virgos live negatively and seek escape from frustrations arising from experiences intended to be their lessons. When living positively Virgos actually place less emphasis on the sexual side of life than do many other people. The organs of the body most influenced by this sign are the solar plexus nerve region and the organs of elimination (bowels, pores and nasal passages). The bowels and skin play a vital role in the health of every person but they are especially important for the Virgo. There is a tendency for them to suffer from clogged pores, creating a dry skin and impeding the elimination of toxic matter through perspiration. The skin's seven million pores also regulate the body's temperature. This function, too, will be inhibited when the pores are clogged by a thickening of the skin's tissue oil. This obstruction is caused by a deficiency in the mineral cell salt Kali Sulph — potassium sulphate. Those toxic wastes which the body cannot adequately eliminate by perspiring are turned back within and must then be processed by the respiratory tract or the bowels. The blocking of the pores also tends to raise the body's temperature, forcing the body to work harder to reprocess the waste matter. This double action further increases the body's temperature, producing what we call colds, accompanied by sluggish bowels. Sometimes this creates the feeling of suffocation, with hot flushes and a craving for cold air. Other symptoms of impaired elimination are catarrhal and asthmatic congestion, severe nerve pains in the region of the solar plexus (particularly painful to Virgo women during their menopause), dandruff, baldness, skin eruptions and conjunctivitis. Foods in which potassium sulphate occurs naturally will greatly assist the body's heroic cleansing efforts. Those richest in the cell salt are:

> green vegetables — especially brussels sprouts and watercress;
> deep sea kelp — powder and granules;
> raw hazelnuts, brazil nuts and chestnuts;
> dried figs and raisins;
> avocado, carrots, corn and eggplant.

Karmic Lesson   Being an Earth Sign, Virgo implies the need for useful service to mankind, necessary for those born under its influence to acquire critical karmic lessons. Suitably achieved through the practice of healing or through the arts, it must always be selfless service. As a Middle Sign, Virgo implies the need for emotional control. They must learn that awareness cannot be achieved when undue emphasis is directed towards the physical body or its lusting for sensational involvements. Freedom, we must remember, is only achieved to the extent that the mind is freed from ignorance and the emotions do not cloud sensitivities.

LIBRA — SEPTEMBER 23 TO OCTOBER 22

Characteristic Expression   Balance is the most noteworthy endowment of people born under this sign, which is symbolised by the scales. The natural inclination of Librans is gentleness, for they are very affectionate individuals with an intense desire to live in peace and harmony and to create such an atmosphere wherever they go. They become utterly disenchanted, above all with dishonest people in public office, finding it impossible to excuse any form of hypocrisy, meanness or shallowness. Librans see marvellous perfection in nature — not the perfection of mathematical symmetry, but the beautiful symphony of the great struggle between the material universe and its elements working inexorably toward order. They especially abhor bloodshed and violence of any type, for such transgression threatens balance and offends beauty. Librans are blessed with a highly perceptive insight and a keen sense of justice, a combination which predisposes them to expressions of frankness often more forthright than flattering. It must be realised that they intend no personal malice by their directness but, rather, seek to correct anything they consider undesirable or outside the appropriate order of things.

Negative Tendencies to be Surmounted   It will be surprising for many people who know Librans to learn that they are naturally peaceful, gentle and affectionate beings. Often negative Librans express themselves in emotional tempestuousness, recklessness and sometimes downright aggressiveness. They also succumb to sexual excesses when their health is unsettled. But it must be emphasised that this is not the natural portrait of a Libran, nor of any well-balanced person. Natural expressive balance is precariously dependent upon the body's chemical balance and when this becomes upset by acidic irritations the brain, nerves and muscles are directly affected. Such internal disharmonies induce

133

actions which are actually in conflict with the individual's real nature. They may become tense, excitable, aggressive or even suicidal in their confusion. Rarely are they aware that internal disharmony is a frequent cause of such unnatural attitudes. Therefore they are not easily convinced that their diet has more influence over their emotions than the environmental factors they prefer to blame, such as the weather, the politicians, the spouse, etc.

Health Aspects
Hyperacidity, in these days of highly processed, non-nutritive foods, is far from uncommon. Most people live with it, believing it to be their natural condition. Consequently, most people tend to be emotionally unstable, easily irritated, readily aggressive. But when this condition prevails for Librans, the departure from their normal and natural mode of expression becomes extreme and critically interferes with their basic purpose in life. One of the most alkalising of the mineral cell salts required by the body is Nat Phos — sodium phosphate. A vital role of this nutrient is to restore the body's chemical balance with its strong alkalinity. Not only must Librans ensure that their diet includes foods rich in this mineral salt, but also they should minimise (preferably avoid) highly processed, acid-forming constituents of the modern diet such as white flour and white sugar products, canned foods, carbonated beverages, tea and coffee, etc. Foods rich in natural sodium phosphate are, in order of concentration:

> egg yolks;
> raw salad vegetables — especially celery, beetroot and carrots;
> brewers yeast;
> dried fruits — especially figs, raisins and sultanas;
> sunflower seed kernels — raw.

Fresh fruit is also an excellent alkalising food and a natural source of high energy fruit sugar (fructose). Each day would be a brighter one if it began with a fresh fruit salad. A daily vegetable salad is also indispensable to Librans to maintain a proper chemical balance. Without such a diet the body will manifest many of the following uncomfortable symptoms of hyperacidity: foul breath, pimples, skin irritations, frontal headaches (often with a feeling of intense cranial pressure), scabby ears which might emit a creamy discharge and feel constantly hot, ulcers, canker sores, rheumatism, diarrhoea and occasional convulsions (especially in children). Parents will also notice that children grind their teeth in sleep if their upper gastrointestinal tract is too acidic. This is often an indication of insufficient fresh fruit and vegetables in the diet. Bodily organs which are especially sensitive for Librans are the kidneys, bladder and adrenal glands — in fact, the entire pelvic region must be carefully looked after to avoid prolapsed organs. Keep the abdominal muscles in good tone by exercise. The lumbar region of the spine is also highly sensitive — lumbago and rheumatism are not uncommon for Librans.

Karmic Lesson   People born under the Sign of Libra are rarely content to pass through life without a marriage partner. For them the pairing of male with female is natural to personal balance and wholeness, as the marital partner serves to supply a counterbalance for the other's limitations. It is through such companionship, as well as through comradeship with others met as they travel through life, that Librans discover the meaning of brotherhood, of sharing and of expanding their awareness of life's purpose for themselves and for all mankind. Brotherhood also teaches emotional control to those Librans who are motivated by the negative tendencies of jealousy, resentment and similarly unbalanced attitudes.

SCORPIO — OCTOBER 23 TO NOVEMBER 22

Characteristic Expression   As the last sign of the emotional, or feeling plane, Scorpio relates to the most feeling, most sensitive parts of the body, viz. the reproductive organs. Hence, so much of the expression of those born under this Sun Sign has its motivation related to sex and to secrecy. The men are more sexually oriented than the women of Scorpio, and therefore are much more emotional; the women are more able to contain their emotions and to direct their energies into paths of healing and creativity. Both men and women have powerful determination and the ability to hide turbulent emotions beneath a facade of apparent calmness. Both are skilful with their hands, a special quality which, when related to their natural healing ability, explains why many are found in the field of health. Both the men and the women make excellent magnetic healers, chiropractors and osteopaths — those who prefer the more conventional aspects of the healing arts gravitate towards surgery and medicine. Their natural sensitivity gives these people reliable intuitive guidance when they are in command of their emotions. Their love of secrecy translates' this power into successful professional conduct.

Negative Tendencies to be Surmounted   Being so impressionable and sensitive, Scorpios must guard against losing command of their feelings and becoming negatively emotional. Scorpio women are far more capable of controlling their emotions than are the men of this sign in early life. Both can, however, achieve successful self-mastery during their years of maturity, although this often has to be forced upon them by necessary emotional lessons involving the heart. These demanding trials are required for the sole purpose of directing their steps further along the Path (towards perfection). During their period of emotional adolescence some Scorpios can become so disturbed that for a time they appear quite bitter and cruel, unreliable and erratic. This is not their true nature, as is evident when personal maturity evolves from self-discipline. Men take longer to achieve this maturity than do women under the Scorpio influence, for which reason marriage between two Scorpios is rarely successful. A note of warning must be given here for Scorpio men: if too much emphasis is directed towards the careless abuse of sex, nervous energy can become seriously depleted. This will be particularly noticeable in the lower limbs, for the sciatic nerves are the most vulnerable. Resulting enervation can predispose towards painful physical constrictions, such as stiffness of the legs and thighs, curvature of the spine, paralysis, premature old age and senility.

Health Aspects
We have already considered some pathological problems affecting Scorpio people as a consequence of their negative living. These are mostly related to the reproductive organs because they are the most sensitive organs in the Scorpio anatomy. Scorpio people have to learn that this region of the body is intended primarily for the begetting of children and for the spontaneous physical expression of overwhelming love between a man and woman. It should not be regarded as a regular playground for over-stimulated desires. The Kundalini, or divine creative force within man, cannot be expressed creatively (upward) and procreatively (downward, or sexually) at the same time. When too frequently involved in procreative expression the Kundalini draws heavily upon the blood's vitality, resulting in a deficiency of the mineral biochemic salt important to Scorpios, Cal Sulph — calcium sulphate. Even if sexual expression is not actually practiced, but is suppressed, almost as much bodily depletion will result. The natural alternative is creative expression, the elevation of the Kundalini into practical service for the betterment of life. So absorbed are the enlightened Scorpios in their creativity that they must take care not to overdo their enthusiasm and drain their nervous energy in this direction by long hours of work with inadequate periods for relaxation. Symptoms of depleted calcium sulphate can be recognised in the body as burning sensations in the feet, anus, stomach, throat, or mouth; sometimes as stomach ulcers, slow-healing wounds, skin ailments and pimples. Loose bowels, not necessarily diarrhoea, can also be the result of insufficient dietary

Cal Sulph. Further evidence of deficiency can be recognised in outward emotional agitation, even before it becomes a source of discomfort within the body. Foods offering important sources of natural calcium sulphate and which should be included in the regular diet of Scorpios are:

> natural cheeses — especially Swiss and cheddar;
> all green vegetables — especially watercress and parsley;
> molasses — but only for people who do not eat sufficient salads;
> raw, unsalted nuts — especially Brazil nuts;
> dried figs;
> raw, fresh egg yolks;
> sunflower seed kernels — raw.

Karmic Lesson   It might seem incongruous that the Sign of Scorpio is on the Emotional Plane yet is one of the Water Triplicity, which implies the general lesson of peace. This indicates that of all the signs, Scorpio implies the most difficult lesson for those born under its influence. This is the lesson of attaining peace by the mastery of the passions and the positive direction of kundalinic energy. Man is not only born under this sign when such a need has been karmically established, but also when his latent ability for healing has to be developed as a positive force in bringing bodily harmony to mankind.

SAGITTARIUS — NOVEMBER 23 TO DECEMBER 22

Characteristic Expression   Particularly characteristic of all healthy Sagittarians is their cheerful, gregarious manner. They are exceptionally goodnatured people who are always fond of company and of involvement in physical activity. Yet they rarely allow people to get too close to them, preferring to maintain a safe distance to ensure their personal freedom. This independence is vital to them, in return they respect its need in other people's lives. Their delight in physical activity extends to many different sports but especially those involving marked athletic ability. Sagittarians invariably possess very strong thighs and can usually move fast on their feet. This, coupled with their gregariousness, indicates why they are more interested in travel and constant movement than they are in static security or deep mental contemplation. When young they tend to shy away from too much responsibility but are prepared to accept their share as they mature. Sagittarians have a deep compassion for all living creatures. They also have a deep natural love of philosophy which they should develop to better understand the purpose of life. Their responsiveness to laws, both those of man and of spirit, invariably results in their accepting both without question or objection. A noteworthy metaphysical quality possessed by most Sagittarians is their prophetic ability to foresee certain events. These sometimes manifest in dreams, but do not always involve them personally. However, disbelief and discouragement when they are young invariably cause them to disregard this faculty. If nurtured this ability could develop into a very powerful endowment, thereby providing considerable benefit to many.

Negative Tendencies to be Surmounted   The desire
for constant change can certainly lead into many and varied avenues of learning; but if allowed to persist unchecked it produces a squandering of mental faculties. Concentration and patience will be weakened unless self-control is adequately exercised. One of the most successful methods of achieving this is by emphasising accuracy in every action. Accuracy is an excellent exercise in care, control and close mental application. Without the acknowledgement and practice of this, the Sagittarian can easily become motivated by idle desire and whim, experiencing many frustrations and, ultimately, loneliness. Symptoms of deterioration will often appear as attitudes sharply alternating between faith and doubt, exhilaration and despondency. Eventually nervous instability will become so intense as to create a highly neurotic person, unless they respond to self-discipline based on those ten valuable exercises in self-enlightenment which Pythagoras called the Mathematical Disciplines*.

Health Aspects   The human body comprises virtually every
known element and it has combined them into a countless number of chemical compounds. The chemicals which make up a building, the soil and the ocean are all similar to those within the body of man, although in different proportions. Even the basic material of glass — sand — is not excluded for it is this mineral, silicon oxide, which is one of the indispensable biochemic cell salts in the body. In fact, silicon oxide is the cell salt which is most important to Sagittarians. Silica, as it is commonly known, is also quartz and is composed of extremely sharp crystals. In this regard, it symbolises the Sagittarian, the archer, with the sharp arrow which pierces its target. When silica is tempered to a high enough point for fusion it becomes crystal clear, as do the thoughts of the Sagittarian when

*See the author's comprehensive health book From Soil to Psyche pp 64-82.

his self-command and awareness have been tempered by the fusion of self-control with adequate experience. Silica is found in the skin and nails of the human body — it gives that natural glossy look to the hair. It is also present in the membrane covering which protects the bones and nerves. In general, this mineral is one of the important strengtheners within the body. An insufficient supply is indicated by difficulty in thinking clearly, by despondency, red eyelids, red nostrils with sore tips, acne and pimples on the face, falling hair, boils, muffled hearing and catarrhal conditions of the upper respiratory tract. Natural foods found to be rich in silica are, in order of available quantity:

> all green vegetables — especially lettuce, parsley, asparagus and cucumber;
> fresh strawberries;
> sunflower seed kernels — raw;
> raw pumpkin seed kernels (pepitas);
> dried figs and sun-dried apricots.

Karmic Lesson   With their natural love of philosophy and their deep compassion for life, Sagittarians are well equipped to develop an excellent level of emotional control and mental stability. This will stand them in good stead for a highly successful life in terms of their relationship with other people. Their natural desire to understand the meaning of things enables them to finely attune to human nature and to provide valuable help to those in need. This is the earthly expression of divine love and the fulfilling of a karmic need common to all Sagittarians.

CAPRICORN — DECEMBER 23 TO JANUARY 21

Characteristic Expression   Caution is the keynote of Capricornian expression. People born under this sign are generally intensely practical — too practical to take risks, or attempt anything about which they have any reservation. Although they have the reputation for being determined, Capricorn people could not be truly regarded as having a strong general determination but rather as being deliberate in doing those things which fall within the ambit of the conventionally acceptable. Being exceptionally law-abiding citizens, they will not go beyond the commonly accepted limitations of conventional society. Consistent with their orthodox attitude to society, these people place great emphasis upon material security, talent and position. Many Capricornians are found at the head of large, established corporations, trusts and syndicates, where they serve very capably and faithfully. Children born when the sun is in Capricorn have very retentive memories but unless they take steps to develop and train their memory, this valuable natural asset will dissipate soon after their academic studies have concluded. Another special aspect of these children is their need for peace — they have a deep inner urge for periods of solitude, without which they could become inexplicably melancholy. In fact, it is quite possible that some of the much-publicised cot deaths are caused by undue noise shattering the delicate emotional balance of infants born under the Sign of Capricorn, especially if they also possess the Arrow of Activity on their Birthcharts (see page 88).

Negative Tendencies to be Surmounted

With the approach of the Aquarian age comes a changing pattern of values in society. The orthodox is being questioned, the conventional is being modified, everything is being investigated as to its suitability for the new age society. This is typically Aquarian, but very un-Capricornian. Consequently, many people born under the Sign of Capricorn are currently feeling insecure because their deep faith in materialism is being shaken. This produces an uneasiness which worries them. Out of this confusion will come a necessary reawakening, a reassessment of their values. They will recognise the important differences between the man made and the natural values in life, between the artificial and the real, the transient and the eternal. Until this realisation brings about the establishment of a new set of values life will seem empty and they will experience much indefinable sadness. They can be easily helped when these causes are recognised for then they will become aware of the need to adjust their outlook and to plan for the future, rather than live in the past.

Health Aspects

Relating Capricorn to the anatomy of man, we find that its emphasis is directed towards the knees and legs. It is, therefore, in this region that special care must be exercised. Caution must be intensified if two or more 4s appear on the Birthchart (see pages 53 and 54). The most abundant mineral salt in the human body is the most critical to the health of Capricornians. Cal Phos — calcium phosphate — is the bone-building material which is important to the health of everyone, but especially to those born under this sign. Most Capricornians are susceptible to weakened bones, to bone and tooth decay (caries) and to excessive albumin in their urine. This free albumin is unable to find sufficient calcium phosphate with which to combine; it consequently overflows into the urine for elimination. The chronic calcium phosphate deficiency symptom of thyroid enlargement which causes the condition known as goitre is not due to lack of iodine but to excessive free albumin. Other calcium phosphate deficiency symptoms which might become evident from time to time are colds and tonsilitis, difficulty in swallowing, periods of hoarseness, irritations in the head and on the face, nervous panic and incapacity for concentrated thought. The orthodox outlook of Capricornians is nowhere more characteristically expressed than in their dietary habits. They follow unquestioningly the modern diet of refined and processed foods, abundant meat and white bread, tea and coffee drinking, snacking on sweets and chocolates, etc. In short, theirs is a diet of limited nutritional value, imposing upon their bodies undesirable acid residues, particularly uric and oxalic acids*. Both these acids leach from the body vital stores of calcium phosphate, creating an inherent problem for people born to follow such habits. Foods affording valuable supplies of natural calcium phosphate are, in descending order of concentration:

brewers and torula yeast;
Swiss and cheddar cheeses;
all raw, unsalted nuts and seeds;
soya beans, soya grits and soya milk;
fresh, unprocessed wheatgerm;
whey powder;
fresh, raw egg yolks;
parsley, broccoli, and most other green vegetables.

Karmic Lesson   As an Earth Sign, Capricorn implies involvement in service to mankind. But first must be attained spiritual understanding to expand the Capricornian outlook. Some find this through their church, some through service clubs, others through charitable work. It is a difficult challenge for Capricornians to recognise the limitations of a material frame of mind. But this they must do if they are to triumph over their dogmatism. In addition they must learn to develop a sensitivity and respect for other people's feelings, at least to the extent that they seek for themselves.

AQUARIUS — JANUARY 22 TO FEBRUARY 20

Characteristic Expression   As harbingers of the new age, Aquarians, not surprisingly, focus on the quality of life and work for the betterment of all living creatures — humanity in particular. It is imperative to the Aquarian that he be allowed to study life in all its grandeur. Such a preoccupation embraces an extremely broad scope

*For detailed information on the effects of these acids within the body, refer to the author's book From Soil to Psyche.

— science, philosophy, religion (comparative, rather than orthodox), mathematics (applied, rather than theoretical) and anything related to veneration for life. This is typically new age. Fundamental to everything Aquarian is his need to be trusted, his need for truth and his abhorrence of hypocrisy. Every Aquarian has an interest in metaphysical concepts which is only now being given full scope in face of mankind's increasingly widened horizons of understanding. As a result the role of the Aquarian is gaining greater importance in society. Blessed with a good memory and a naturally strong fortitude, Aquarians have always been the seekers of esoteric knowledge; but now they are coming into their own powerful era when such knowledge is not only accepted, but actually sought after.

Negative Tendencies to be Surmounted
Arising from their intense dislike of deception and hypocrisy, Aquarians are apt to over-react against those whom they regard as guilty of such conduct. It is then that they must remind themselves that life is full of lessons and that the hypocrite, by perpetrating such a sin, has initiated his own karmic retribution which will manifest as his appropriate lesson at precisely the right time. However, the Aquarian should be ever ready to offer him compassionate guidance and brotherly love. An emotional reaction on the part of the Aquarian would commit errors for which he would have to pay a karmic debt. The Aquarian suffers acutely from tensions, due to his highly sensitive nervous system and delicate digestive system. Frequent headaches are the usual consequence. Other symptoms of emotional tension include impaired blood circulation, depression and constant tiredness — all the result of enervation. Aquarians must recognise that their acute sensitivities are intended to facilitate the understanding of life (both physically and metaphysically). Along with this they must learn to protect themselves from those who would impose on them and waste their vital energy, or attempt to regulate and exploit their powers. Such understanding demands careful training in the Mathematical Disciplines of Pythagoras — those exercises in enlightenment which equip man for his greatest achievement, empire over the self, as Pythagoras described it.

Health Aspects
The expression of the Aquarian reveals itself more in mental and spiritual than physical realms. They should, therefore, not try to emulate feats of physical prowess performed by others, but be content with their own special powers. Aquarians have certain vulnerable parts of their bodies which require special care. These are the ankles, calves and neck. It follows that they should avoid skiing, football and other sports or activities in which these parts of the body are placed in jeopardy. Aquarians generally have slender necks and will often register tension in this region,

causing headaches or backpains requiring chiropractic care. The biochemic cell salt most needed by Aquarians is Nat Mur — sodium chloride. This is usually referred to as common salt and is the second most plentiful salt in the body. But the sodium chloride demanded by the body as a component of cellular nutrition is certainly not the common salt originating in seawater. Sea salt and table salt are far too coarse for the body's use because they irritate the highly sensitive linings of the gastrointestinal tract. Its addition to food will often lead to hypertension, swollen joints and other problems involving the blood and the joints. Man must obtain his basic nutrients from the soil of which his body originally derived, as the Bible tells us and science confirms. Natural foods rich in sodium chloride are headed by green vegetables, especially celery, beetroot and carrots. Also included in the list are dried figs, raisins and sultanas; for those who seek additional sources, egg yolk, brewers yeast and molasses can be taken. Deficiency in natural sodium chloride can cause impaired digestion due to lack of mucus, dry mouth and throat, irritation of the eyes and skin, chilblains and reduced vitality. Contrary to popular belief cramps do not arise from inadequate sodium chloride but rather from inadequate circulation and or excessive cellular toxicity. Ingesting salt tablets after excessive perspiration defeats the body's efforts to rid itself of this unwanted saline toxicity through its pores.

Karmic Lesson   The role of the Aquarian as preparer for the new age is already well known. This is achieved through the building of a strong bond of kinship uniting all mankind in tolerant respect for the individual; for human society is a huge conglomeration of people of vastly differing spiritual ages, karmic histories, geographical limitations, ethnic origins and religious conditionings. Total guidance can, therefore, never be achieved by a rigid, dogmatic plan. Human betterment will result only from individualised understanding which, in turn, permits the best development of the individual. But the essential ingredient to all this is brotherhood: the recognition that the ideal fraternity of the new age is based on the harmonising of individual personalities for the uplifting of all.

PISCES — FEBRUARY 21 TO MARCH 20

Characteristic Expression   Some of the sweetest, kindest people put on earth are born under the sign of Pisces. These people seem to possess a special talent for helping those in need, considerably assisted by their hypersensitive nature. They are very

143

responsive to environmental influences and, therefore, should not knowingly expose themselves to hostile conditions. The loyalty, trustworthiness and generosity of a well-adjusted Piscean are obvious to all who know them. It is because they are so willing that they are easily imposed upon and should learn to guard against this. Pisceans should not assume that everyone is as trustworthy as they are. The natural loving sympathy of people born under the sign of Pisces makes them ideal healers. Whether the demand be of a physical, emotional or psychic nature, they will understand and provide the help where it is most needed. Again, they do not regard this quality as anything special, believing everyone to be so endowed. This illustrates the beautiful, natural modesty of the Piscean — an unusual quality in these years of acute ambitiousness. Dedicated to helping mankind, the efficient and industrious Pisceans tend to overlook the less worthy motives of many with fewer scruples. They must learn to sharpen their powers of assessment and to discriminate between those souls who really need their help and those who merely want it because it is easier than helping themselves.

Negative Tendencies to be Surmounted
The lack of sound judgement which characterises younger Pisceans must often be remedied by hurtful experiences. It seems unfortunate that their acute sensitivity has to be so harshly treated, but so essential are life's lessons that no other method will suffice. As they develop a little more confidence, Pisceans become prone to overanxiety about those in need. No matter how much they do to help, they are invariably troubled by the thought that they are not doing enough. This anxiety can become a real problem to them unless they adopt a more philosophic understanding, supported by adequate training in as many of the natural therapies as they can assimilate. Unless they secure a sound training, in their enthusiasm to heal Pisceans could unwittingly dissipate their energies and become despondent. This could lead them away from harsh reality to seek solace in drugs, alcohol or crime. Some suffer from long-term mental derangement as a result of many and repeated frustrations.

Health Aspects
The bodily extremities of the Piscean are of pronounced importance — they have strong healing hands, but weak feet. There is a powerful magnetic healing force natural to Pisceans which is capably transmitted through their hands. Their feet often cause them anguish from strains, sprains, fallen arches and the like, indicating they must take special care of these vital appendages. The biochemic cell salt indispensable to the health of Pisceans is Ferrum Phos — ferric (iron) phosphate. As iron attracts oxygen, this vital mineral salt revitalises the body by energising the blood. Simultaneously it carries essential oxygen around the body for use

in its every function. If insufficient oxygen is available in the blood the body attempts to distribute the ration as best it can. To do this the blood motion (pressure) is increased. This creates higher-than-normal internal heat, often high enough to be called fever. Rather than treat this fever with suppressant drugs, the content of ferric phosphate should be increased by ensuring that the diet comprises foods rich in this nutrient. If the correction is not undertaken the more chronic problem of anemia can result. Further symptoms of deficiency in ferric phosphate include depression, bleeding, inflammatory pains and congestion. This is such a vital salt that its deficiency affects the functioning of every part of the body. A wide choice of natural foods rich in ferric phosphate, listed in order of concentration, are:

> brewers and torula yeasts;
> pepitas (Mexican pumpkin seed kernels), sunflower seed kernels;
> soya beans, soya grits and soya milk;
> wheatgerm and bran;
> fresh, raw nuts — especially almonds, pistachios and pine nut kernels;
> egg yolk — fresh, preferably raw;
> sprouted seeds, pulses and grains.

Karmic Lesson

This sign is the one which offers most peace. Yet we are passing through what has been universally regarded as the Piscean age without appearing to have achieved much peace in the world. Other quite tremendous factors, based on human craving for power and fame, seemed to intercede, placing greater demand upon the forthcoming Aquarian age to improve the quality of life on earth. Pisceans are destined to play a unique role in this endeavour for they are eminently qualified to teach the world peace through understanding and trust. By the same token they are intended to bring peace to those sick people whose illnesses have hindered their eternal search for the Inner Self.

A QUICK-REFERENCE CHART

SUN SIGN	PHYSICAL CHARACTERISTICS	PERSONALITY CHARACTERISTICS	NEGATIVE ASPECTS	BIOCHEMIC CELL SALT	HEALTH PROBLEMS	KARMIC LESSON
ARIES	large head and brain	mentally active, courageous, volatile	impatient, critical, hot tempered	potassium phosphate KH_2PO_4	headaches, hyper-acidity	emotional control, selfless love
TAURUS	strong neck, powerful voice, large ears	strong, active, very stable, reliable	gluttonous, obstinate, overindulgent	sodium sulphate Na_2SO_4	water retention, liver upsets, toxicity	selfless service, control of desires
GEMINI	strong hands, arms and shoulders	fast thinking, highly sensitive, dual natured	very reactive, nervous, insecure	potassium chloride KCl	respiration, congestion, menstrual problems	brotherhood
CANCER	weak stomach and chest, healing hands	persistent, prudent, homeloving	moody, shy, fearful	calcium fluoride CaF_2	cracked skin, tooth decay, gastritis	inner peace through self-control
LEO	nervousness, alertness	affectionate, energetic, self-motivated	hot tempered, reckless, sexual	magnesium phosphate $MgHPO_4$	weak heart, nerve spasms, cramps	spirituality of love
VIRGO	sluggish bowels, dry skin	seek perfection, reliable, generous	hypercritical, overanxious, hyperchondriacal	potassium sulphate K_2SO_4	colds, fevers, constipation, skin ailments	service through healing
LIBRA	gentleness, tender abdomen	balanced, just, frank	reckless, aggressive, tense	sodium phosphate Na_2HPO_4	hyperacidity, ulcers, rheumatism	brotherhood through sharing marriage
SCORPIO	reproductive organs, skilful hands	determined, secretive, composed	sexual, agitated, erratic	calcium sulphate $CaSO_4$	skin ailments, blood toxicity, ulcers	creative self-control
SAGITTARIUS	strong thighs, fast movement	cheerful, independent, compassionate	unstable, frustrated, lonely	silicon oxide SiO_2	skin eruptions, brittle nails, scalp disorders	understanding and helping the needy
CAPRICORN	weak knees and legs	orthodox, determined, practical	materialistic, insecure, fearful, dogmatic	calcium phosphate $CaHPO_4$	weak bones and teeth, excess albumin	spiritual understanding through service
AQUARIUS	weak ankles and neck	trusting, honest, truth seekers, forbearing	hypersensitive, reactive, nervous	sodium chloride NaCl	tiredness, indigestion, headaches	awareness through brotherhood
PISCES	healing hands, weak feet	loyal, generous, sympathetic	frustrated, anxious, despondent	iron phosphate $FePO_4$	hypertension, inflamations, fevers	peace through understanding and trust

STAGE 12
The Power of Names

One of the most sacred sounds to people's ears is their name. Doubtless you have noticed that, no matter how noisy the surroundings, when someone calls your name your attention is instantly diverted to them.

Our names have become a very important sound to us, whether it be our given names, our pet names, our nick-names, or whatever appellations we prefer to use. Acutally, our names must be regarded as an adopted part of our personality and expression. A name is important because its vibrations become fused with our own. The term vibration implies not only the audible wave frequencies but, even more broadly, the symbolic vibrations of the name as indicated by its numerological pattern. These vibrations exert an influence on our very personality and individuality, as schematically indicated by the chart on page 5.

Many people overlook the influence exerted by their name on the overall expression of their personality, but let us not dismiss this subject too hastily. Names are not given to us by chance or by accident. They attach themselves to us according to our need, although we are rarely aware of this. Parents will choose a name for their child guided by some preference. What created that preference? Nothing occurs by chance — there is always a reason, whether we are aware of it or not. Likewise, there is always a reason for those who change their name — often a far deeper reason than initially suspected. Numerologically, we can reveal that reason and, in so doing, we discover a deeper side to our personality.

Reasons for selecting names can occupy an entire book of fascinating reading. But we are more immediately in need of understanding the influence of our name as it now relates to our individuality. This will throw further light upon the discovery of the Inner Self.

The force exerted by names on the moulding of personalities will primarily depend upon the strength of the name and its relationship to the Ruling Number of the people. If they have a less-than-powerful birthdate the influence of their name will be far greater

147

than if the reverse applied. This is particularly exemplified in the life of the sixteenth president of the United States of America, Abraham Lincoln. His birthdate (February 12, 1809) was not powerful, but his name gave the strength he needed to overcome personality weaknesses and achieve a lasting place in history. By contrast, a powerful birthdate, such as December 27, 1935, and the name John will find very little influence exercised upon personality by the name. Analysis will support this contention.

Irrespective of age, all people respond to some degree to the vibrations of their names. This response is greatest during the impressionable years of infancy and adolescence. Indeed, it can be of great help to children if parents are numerologically guided in their selection of the children's names. Names which are chosen for balanced power can be far more beneficial to the children than names with conflicting vibrations. Personalities will be more balanced if name and birthdate harmonise.

To assess the power of a name we must start by obtaining its numerological values. This is achieved by translating the letters of the name to their equivalent numbers, using the following table:

1	2	3	4	5	6	7	8	9
A	B	C	D	E	F	G	H	I
J	K	L	M	N	O	P	Q	R
S	T	U	V	W	X	Y	Z	

There is no immediate need to memorise this table, for the numerical equivalent of each letter will become readily recognised with practice. As A is the first letter of the alphabet, it is equivalent to the first number of the numerical scale, the number 1. Each successive letter after A relates to the equivalent number following 1. Thus, B is equivalent to 2, C to 3, D to 4 and so on to the last letter of the alphabet.

At this point many people ask: "But how does this system relate to another language?" Experience proves that relationships do exist between the alphabetical and numerical systems of every culture. However, first let us become totally familiar with this method in our native language. Then, if we have the time and patience, we can expand our knowledge to a numerological understanding of another language.

When analysing names we are concerned only with the used names. It is of little more than academic interest to analyse a given name or a family name if it is not used by the person. Even if a name is changed by contraction, for professional or any other reasons, our interest lies in analysing whatever name is used in daily life. For instance, Allen might prefer to be called Al, William might prefer Bill, Samuel might prefer Mark (as in Samuel Clemens' case) or Sam.

In other instances people have been known to dislike their first name, preferring to be known by their middle name. Others might dislike both their first and middle names, preferring to be known only by the initials of both. This is popular in southern U.S.A. where, for instance, a person called Jacob Benjamin might wish to be known simply as J.B. — we would then analyse JB as his first name.

The analysis of rejected names will often throw an interesting light on the personalities by indicating the reason for the change. There might also be environmental reasons associating that name with other persons, places or social attitudes which they dislike. These, also, can often be numerologically explained. It is always illuminating to compare the reason given by people for the change with that revealed by numerological analysis.

Whatever the reason given by those persons, it is clear that the name they use is the one we must analyse, for used names are living names and only living names have vibrational influence on the Inner Self.

Practice will reveal that a different degree of emphasis will exist between persons' used first name and their family name (surname). As a rule, the first name is used more in personal affairs, so it has greater impact on the personality. Family names are used more frequently in business or professional circles, hence their greater influence in these fields. These points should be recognised when the analysis is being made.

In translating the name to its numerological equivalent we adopt a simple method of separating the numbers of the consonants from those of the vowels. This enables us to easily obtain the totals of vowel numbers and consonant numbers separately. From the separate totals, we can gain an understanding of the name's influence on the personality in terms of its soul urge (vowels) and its outer expression (consonants). Then by adding these two totals we obtain the ruling number equivalent of the name, the Complete Name Number. Please note that a double first name (eg: Sally Anne) or a hyphenated surname are to be analysed as one name.

Examples of the following three names will indicate how the upper line of numbers represents the vowels of each name. When totalled, these provide the Soul Urge Number. The lower line of numbers represents the consonants and, by their totals, the Outer Expression Number is obtained, as shown:

```
      1    1    1    3
    A B R A H A M      26/8
      2 9    8    4  23/5


      5   9   1   5      20/2
    E L I Z A B E T H        43/7
      3   8   2   2 8  23/5


      6    6
    J O H N    20/2
    1   8 5  14/5
```

SOUL URGE NUMBERS

In the same manner as the individual numbers of the birthdate are added to obtain the Ruling Number, individual numbers of each vowel in a name are added to obtain the Soul Urge Number. As indicated by the vowel numbers in the three above examples the Soul Urge Number of the name Abraham is 3; Elizabeth is 2; John is 6. This method is followed for each of the used names of a person.

Vowels are the soul of a word, its life, so to speak. Every trained singer, actor and speaker recognises this. It is therefore apparent that the vowel numbers of a person's name bear a close relationship to that person's inner feelings, the nature of which is discernible from the total of the vowel numbers, known appropriately as the Soul Urge Number.

From the Soul Urge Number of a given name we learn some of the more subtle aspects of the individual's spiritual sensitivities, fortitude and drive. These can be expressed in a variety of manners: by feelings, emotions, desires, fancies, etc. The forms of expression will vary with each Soul Urge Number.

A basic guide of the qualities indicated by each of the eleven Soul Urge Numbers follows:

Soul Urge 1
This appears only in names containing the single vowel 'a': Ann, Jack, Sally and Chad. The need for individual freedom of expression is indicated here. The means by which this is to be achieved will be demonstrated best by the person's Ruling Number. In general this Soul Urge Number implies a strong desire for freedom in the form of sufficient time to themselves, either to relax or to

undertake some kind of personal artistic expression.

Soul Urge 2
Representative names are Anna, Elizabeth, Adam, Oliver — vowel numbers total either 2 or 20. Here is an urge to do things in a balanced way so that harmony prevails in every expression. These are generally quite intuitive people, with a strong preference for the natural over the artificial. In their dealings with other people they are very fair and, by the same token, expect the same in return.

Soul Urge 3
Representative names are Amanda, Joanne, Chuck — vowel numbers total 3, 12 or 21. With its emphasis always anchored on the mental level, 3 as a Soul Urge Number combines feeling with thinking and with assessing. The result is generally a capable appraisal of people and situations. This can be highly beneficial in business and professional activities.

Soul Urge 4
Representative names are Stuart, Una, Angus, Paul — vowel numbers total either 4 or 13. When the practical 4 is expressed at the soul level it indicates that the individual has very orderly conservative opinions on a wide range of spiritual and emotional subjects embracing religion, love, marriage and life in general. They are usually quite orthodox in outlook and not given to emotional outbursts.

Soul Urge 5
Representative names are Betty, Shirley, Keith, Kelly — vowel numbers total either 5 or 14. With its natural strength derived from being located on the Soul Plane, the occurrence of 5 as a Soul Urge Number implies great depth of feeling and the need for freedom and acceptance, the better to express such feelings. Whatever the aspect of life involved these people will invariably feel strongly about it and will have their say regarding it (unless some strong inhibitions are present in the Birthchart, such as the Arrow of Hypersensitivity).

Soul Urge 6
Representative names are Charles, Allen, Megan, Jane — vowel numbers total either 6 or 15. Love and creativity are the operative words here. Every opportunity to express creative faculties should be grasped, whether at work, with a hobby, or in the home. This strength will decline into despair and torment if they lapse into overanxiety.

Soul Urge 7
Representative names are Joan, Angela, Hamilton, Marianne — vowel numbers total either 7 or 16. The urge to teach and to help others is the predominant driving force here. However, they do not take too kindly to others teaching them, preferring to learn by their own experiences. They often pay dearly for this privilege until they come to the realisation that human beings are intended to help each other in a two-way relationship.

Soul Urge 8   Representative names are Joanna, Bruce, Jonathan — vowel numbers total either 8 or 17. More than wishing to act independently, these people tend to mentally disassociate from conventionally accepted habits, if such habits do not seem reasonable to them. They evidence a strong preference for individual thought and freedom but must guard against becoming aloof. One important lesson life teaches us is the need to participate in society without necessarily being bound by it.

Soul Urge 9   Representative names are Samuel, Claude, Phyllis — vowel numbers total 9 or 18. When living positively these people always seek to improve the quality of life, guided by a keen sense of humanitarian responsibility. If living negatively they tend to become overly ambitious, with an unbalanced idealism which nags them into many egocentric (and often unsuccessful) acts. The power of this number should be respected and utilised altruistically, otherwise it can become a savage taskmaster.

Soul Urge 10   Representative names are Lisa, Craig, David, Douglas — vowel numbers total either 10 or 19. Metaphysical flexibility is the power conferred by this number. It offers the ability to bring into play a wide range of soul-oriented powers. Putting to use such metaphysical endowments as intuition, clairvoyance, clairaudience, thought transference and astral projection will negate many of the limitations society places on its numbers to suppress the expression of human individuality. To employ any of these faculties in daily life constructively emancipates these people from the earth-bound state and brings awareness of the divinity within man, the essence of life.

Soul Urge 11   Representative names are Robert, Errol, Cleo — vowel numbers total 11 only. The special spiritual qualities of the 11 are apparent here. As a Soul Urge Number it offers a valuable intuitive strength which is especially beneficial if the persons have not already gained intuitiveness from the Birthchart or Ruling Number. It also serves to increase compassion and ability to attune to other people's feelings.

HOW TO ANALYSE THE Y

Numerologically, the Y is usually considered a consonant, with the value of 7. It will ordinarily appear as an Outer Expression Number, exemplified in such names as Kelly, Sally and Shirley. However, the exception arises in a name in which the Y is pronounced as 'i' or 'e' with no actual vowel appearing in the name. Then, and only then, do we analyse the Y as a vowel, thereby giving the name a Soul Urge

Number of 7, as in Lyn, Ty, or the surnames of Byrd, Hynd, Kydd and Lynch.

OUTER EXPRESSION NUMBERS

Obtaining the value of the Outer Expression Number of each name follows the same pattern already established for Soul Urge Numbers. By adding together the numerical values of the consonants below the name (as shown in the examples on page 150), their total is readily obtained, then easily converted to its single digit equivalent which we now recognise as the Outer Expression Number. Again referring to the previous examples on page 150, we find that for the three names chosen for numerological conversion each has, coincidentally, an Outer Expression Number of 5.

The Soul Urge Numbers range from 1 through to 11. The same holds true for the Outer Expression Numbers, except for the additional number of 22/4. Experience has shown that names in the English language possess insufficient vowels to total 22; however it is not uncommon to find names with the correct proportion of consonants to give this total.

Characteristics associated with each of the Outer Expression Numbers of names are:

Outer Expression 1   This can only occur in names with the single consonant of J or S to give a consonant number total of 1 only. Few given names comply with this limitation but among those which do Sue and Joe are the most commonly used. The trait most notably expressed by this number is exemplified by the solo sportsman or solo worker. They are people who need the freedom to set their own pace in order to achieve greatest satisfaction and to develop their self-confidence in physical activities.

Outer Expression 2   Examples of names are Samantha, Jose, Nicholas — names with consonant number totals of either 2 or 20. Indicated here is the preference to work in company as part of a group in happy surroundings. They are bright people with a desire for fun and light-hearted pleasures. This does not imply that they are shallow, but rather that they have a great capacity to enjoy organised activity.

Outer Expression 3   Examples of names are David, Keith, Jody, Beth — names with consonant number totals of 3, 12, 21 or 30. Whereas the Outer Expression Number of 2 reveals a person who enjoys being entertained, the 3 reveals himself as the entertainer. They derive great pleasure and give as much to others by being the life of the party, for they usually have a quick wit and a bright outlook.

153

Outer Expression 4 Examples of names are Eloise, Betty, Angus — names with consonant number totals of 4, 13 or 31. This is an intensely practical number, belonging to doing people who always seek involvement with their hands, feet or bodies. They specifically enjoy sports and building or repairing things.

Outer Expression 5 Examples of names are Ian, Sally, Stuart, Bruce — names with consonant number totals of 5, 14, 23 or 32. Freedom from physical confinement is the oft-expressed need of these people. Yet they sometimes allow misunderstandings or shyness to inhibit the fullness of their expression. To avoid such frustrations they should seek an unconfining job and the company of those with whom they feel at ease — to put it simply, they need the company of responsive, uninhibited people.

Outer Expression 6 Examples of names are James, Jane, Douglas, Angela — names with consonant number totals of 6, 15, 24 or 33. The tendency to focus much of their energies and attention on the home is the ever present characteristic here. Of course, this might appear to have very decided advantages for the family, but it can also spoil them. Caution must be used to avoid over-indulgence by maintaining a practical balance between pampering and attending to the more realistic needs of the domestic circle.

Outer Expression 7 Examples of names are Oliver, Philip, Megan, Chuck — names with consonant number totals of 7, 16, 25 or 34. These people have the compulsion for doing things themselves, being strongly motivated toward personal involvement and learning on their own terms and in their own way. They much prefer a personal sense of achievement and the satisfaction of discovering for themselves to the more amenable course of learning from others.

Outer Expression 8 Examples of names are Adam, Samuel, Bill — names with consonant number totals of 8, 17, 26 or 35. We find here a very strong desire for independent expression. These are people who elect to act individualistically, to the extent that they dare to be different if the need demands it. In this manner they assert their strong personalities, for they are aware that man can never achieve a high level of self-development when identified with the herd mind.

Outer Expression 9 Examples of names are Sarah, Pat, Don — names with consonant number totals of 9, 18, 27 or 36. There is no denying that life has its serious and its humorous sides. A balanced personal life is one in which the two successfully interrelate. Unhappily, people with this Outer Expression Number tend to over-emphasise the seriousness of life. In so doing they attract sadness and sometimes loneliness, the result of not considering the lighter side of life of sufficient importance to be bothered with it. Their capacity for deep contemplation and penetrative analysis and for the implementation of their high ideals are fine virtues, but they must be balanced with a little light pleasure to revitalise mind and body.

Outer Expression 10   Examples of names are Craig, Paul, Shirley, Claude, Ann — names with consonant number totals of 10, 19, 28 or 37. Outer expression traits indicated by this number are virtually the opposite of those applying to the 9. The inclination to guard against here is that of becoming too flippant and superficial, when the real function of this number is adaptation to life's varying circumstances and situations. People with this Outer Expression Number should be prepared to exert greater determination to fulfil their role in life, for only by balancing seriousness with lightness will they achieve success.

Outer Expression 11   Examples of names are Allan, Joanne, Jonathan — names with consonant number totals of either 11 or 29. The predominant need here is for harmony. Indicated by this Outer Expression Number is balanced spiritual and emotional expression. Its special purpose is to instil a longing to harmonise surroundings, control emotions and develop and share a deepened understanding of life. It is only by following this path that the individual will be led through the gates of happiness.

Outer Expression 22/4   Examples of names are Hamilton, Robert — those few names with a consonant number total of 22 only. We know this to be an exceptionally strong power for organising, especially in business and commercial ventures. If the person's Ruling Number is a 4, 8 or 22/4, special care must be taken to maintain a balance in his activities, for the strong leaning here is towards an over-emphasis on moneymaking, almost to the point of obsession. Even for people with other Ruling Numbers, the same advice will apply: endeavour to expand your organisational activities into other than commercial fields by working in such compassionate fields as worthy charities, particularly those benefiting under-privileged children if you wish to gain a balanced equilibrium.

COMPLETE NAME NUMBERS

The third aspect of the numerology of names is the key to the name's general strength. This is known as the Complete Name Number. It is related to, but less powerful than, the Ruling Number.

The Complete Name Number is obtained by adding together all

the numbers of a name in both the first name and surname, then totalling them in the same manner as was done to obtain the Ruling Number. Referring again to our original examples on page 150, the Complete Name Number of Abraham is 8, Elizabeth is 7, and John is 2.

Complete Name Numbers range in value from 2 through to 11 and then 22/4. The extent of the influence of the Complete Name Number lies in its relationship to the Ruling Number, rather than any specific contribution of its own. A Complete Name Number can either balance or reinforce the power of the Ruling Number. If it is numerically the same as the Ruling Number it offers the greatest reinforcement to the Ruling Number. If the Complete Name Number is different to the Ruling Number, but on the same plane (4, 7 and 10 on the Physical Plane; 2, 5, 8 and 11 on the Spiritual Plane; 3, 6 and 9 on the Mental Plane — 22/4 is both on the Physical and Spiritual Planes), balancing reinforcement is given on that plane.

Finally, if a Complete Name Number is on a different plane to the Ruling Number, a wider range of vibrations is provided for the broadening of the personality.

NAMECHART

Analysing the Soul Urge, Outer Expression and Complete Name Numbers of people's names will provide an understanding of some of the post-natal influences exercised by the names. A chart of a name, similar to that drawn up for the birthdate (pages 41 to 44), will unveil further aspects of its contribution to the development of the personality.

The number equivalent of a name's individual letters is placed in its correct space on the chart to show the pattern of the name. To examplify this we shall use the three sample names from page 150 and construct their Namecharts:

```
  1   1 1 1
  A B R A H A M
  2 9   8   4
```

		9
2		8
111	4	

```
  5 9 1 5
  E L I Z A B E T H
  3 8 2 2 8
```

3		9
22	55	88
1		

```
        6
  J O H N
  1 8 5
```

	6	
	5	8
1		

156

The name pattern is a distinct help in more fully evaluating the personality. When we place both charts (one for each operative name) beside the Birthchart, we look for the relationship between the Namecharts on the one hand, and the Birthchart on the other. (The interrelation of the two Namecharts is of little significance to any but the most advanced student.)

Close examination of the juxtaposed Name and Birthcharts shows that there are three possibilities to look for:

Does the Namechart offer any strengths which balance weaknesses on the Birthchart? This is the most desirable function of the Namechart. For instance, if the Birthchart had the Arrow of Hypersensitivity (no 2, 5, 8) and the Namechart supplied the Arrow of Emotional Balance (2, 5 and 8), we have the most desirable balance. If the Namechart only had one or two numbers on the Spiritual Plane this could still provide some valuable balance.

Does the Namechart intensify any strength already present on the Birthchart? This creates the most undesirable combination. For instance, if the Namechart possessed any of the same arrows as the Birthchart, or if it had an abundance of the same numbers as those already appearing on the Birthchart, there would be too great a concentration of strength. Wherever you have an over-concentration of power you will always find compounded weaknesses — balance is much more desirable. Remember that the Birthchart cannot be changed but the name can. In these instances it is wise to look to a modification in the structure of the name to try to provide better balance.

Does the name do nothing for the Birthchart? From time to time this predicament presents itself. This occurs when a Namechart cannot offer significant strength to balance weaknesses on the Birthchart, or when the same weaknesses prevail on both charts. In either case the name is providing neither advantage nor disadvantage. Yet often, with a slight change in spelling, alteration in length or interchange of names, definite advantages can develop to provide harmony and balance. Alternatively, a total name change should be considered.

To illustrate with an easy-to-follow example, we shall take one of the first names previously used as an illustration and the birthdate of a person suited to give it striking pertinency — Queen Elizabeth II, born April 21, 1926.

157

4 - 21 - 1926 = 25/7

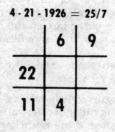

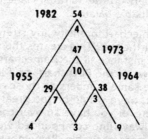

PYRAMIDS

The most noticeable similarity is that her Ruling Number and Complete Name Number are both 7. This strengthens the Ruling Number, indicating the need for the greater strength to undergo many personal sacrifices in early years to attain her impressive level of adjustment and self-control, as well as her ability to impart guidance to others.

The plane of strongest expression here is the Spiritual Plane. It indicates balanced intuition and sensitivity (the two 2s on the Birthchart supported by a doubling of the Arrow of Emotional Balance on the Namechart). Further spiritual strength comes from the Soul Urge and Outer Expression Numbers of the name (2 and 5 respectively), as they are both spiritual numbers.

The Mental Plane of the Queen's Birthchart is also strong and well-balanced, for although it is devoid of the 3 this is compensated for by her Day Number 3. Added mental balance is indicated by the top line of her Namechart.

Her combination of mental and spiritual balance, together with her capability in self-expression (as indicated by the two 1s on her Birthchart), disclose her natural ease in communicating just what and how much Queen Elizabeth wishes to reveal (the double Arrow of Emotional Balance on the Namechart). But her Ruling Number 7 and Complete Name Number 7 indicate that she had much to learn about what should and should not be said in her public appearances. She found such conforming difficult because she felt that it curtailed her freedom.

No arrows of strength appear on her Birthchart. However, her strongest inherent guidance derives from her intuition. This is reinforced by the two 2s on her Namechart which are in the centre of the Arrow of the Planner (arrow 1-2-3).

It will be helpful to students of numerology to observe some further points of importance in the personality of Queen Elizabeth:

Ruling 7 people are usually among the most truthful and honest to be found. This virtue is especially apparent here, for Queen Elizabeth takes her position as Protector of the Faith very seriously, employing uncompromising sincerity to try to live up to the ethics of her church. Hypocrisy is abhorrent to her, hence the conflicts within her family must have upset her when the subject of her sister's divorce arose. Such disharmonies are felt very deeply by the Queen due to her strong sense of family responsibility (indicated by the 6 and 9 together without a 3 on her Birthchart).

So many factors about the Queen's charts and Pyramids indicate that life to her is a very serious business. She has little time or patience with flippancy. Her strong Spiritual Planes and the numbers about the Peaks of her Pyramids show that she is a person who would never shirk her responsibilities. In fact, the 9 as the last number on the base of her Pyramids, indicates that she has even more responsibilities to face in the final stage of her life, the fulfilment.

Her alert intuition (the double 2s), combined with the Ruling Number 7 and Complete Name Number 7, is a very reliable indicator of her approach to making decisions. No doubt many of the Queen's advisers have complained that she does not consult them as often as she should. In her mind she does not need to. And now that she has passed the third Peak on her Pyramids, her maturity is so well developed that she could probably be of more guidance to her advisers than they to her.

The doubling of the 1s and 2s on her Birthchart indicate how capably the Queen can appreciate other people's viewpoints. She can readily comprehend both sides of a contentious matter — an important attribute when dealing so much with public figures, especially politicians.

The seriousness of her regal position occupies so much of Queen Elizabeth's consciousness that she needs encouragement to allow some diversion into her life. Prince Philip, with his highly developed sense of humour, is especially helpful in this regard. With his encouragement, the Queen does not take long to discover her

159

other self through her Day Number 3. The further influence of her Outer Expression Number 5 reveals that she has the ability to enjoy light entertainment and desires to be free to indulge in that enjoyment from time to time.

An analysis of Prince Philip's name and date of birth (June 10, 1921) provides an excellent exercise for the student. From this it can be seen how much dedicated support he has given the Queen and how much it has assisted her to ease so graciously into her high position in public life. It will also become clear how well suited the Queen and her husband are. Without his support, her acute sensitivity could have led Queen Elizabeth to become somewhat withdrawn.

This is not intended to be an exhaustive analysis, but rather an indication of the interrelationship between the various aspects of numerology. The Queen was chosen as an example because of her worldwide fame and single name. Under normal circumstances we have at least two used names to analyse for a person — if they are in show business or have taken a pseudonym for professional reasons, we must also analyse those to ascertain the relationships between the various names as well as the birthdate characteristics.

CHOOSING A SUITABLE NAME

From the foregoing analysis it is clear how helpful the name Elizabeth is to the Queen. When we analyse successful people we find this to be a consistent fact: almost without exception, their name will be in harmony with, and a source of strength to, their natal powers.

What forces operate on the consciousness of a couple or an individual to direct their choice of a name for the newborn babe? Rarely does a person consider it necessary to consult a numerologist to have desirable names analysed; yet such a practice would greatly assist development of the child's individuality by creating more harmony between the natal characteristics and those of the name.

In practice, we find some surprisingly inspired instances of parents who unconsciously chose ideal names for their children. It is as though they were strongly impressed to choose such names by some power of which they have little or no cognisance. Unfortunately these circumstances are in the minority for all too often we find that people have names which create something short of ideal harmony or balance for their personality. Some people have themselves recognised this problem and have changed their used name with subsequent success. This often occurs in the acting and literary professions.

Some years ago, an attractive young lady came to me for advice as to how she could improve her acting and so obtain better parts in television movies and plays. She had heard that it was numerologically possible to change one's name to bring about 'better luck', as she called it. Up until then, this lady had only managed to gain work in television commercials, but she so wanted to play romantic roles in dramatic shows.

An analysis of her numerology revealed that a key aspect of her problem was the Arrow of Hypersensitivity on her Birthchart, with no counteracting strength from either her Ruling Number (which was 6) or her Namechart or Soul Urge Numbers. This inhibited her emotional expression.

The remedy was to advise her of a name change. In so doing, I had her choose alternative stage names which felt comfortable to her. (It is important to do this, as the client will be the one who has to constantly use the new name.) From the list she gave me on the next visit, I chose one which stood out clearly as offering her an improved balanced expression for her sensitivity in conjunction with the vibrant creative power offered by her ruling 6. She liked the new name and immediately commenced to use it professionally.

Within a month, this lady had obtained an important role in a new television romantic drama. It was not the lead, but she soon had an unexpected leading role coming up. So convincing was her romantic acting that she had the producer of the play fall in love with her — and she with him. They married the following year and now she plays the starring role in her lovely home, where she has two beautiful young children and a very devoted husband.

As people become more aware of the important role of the name in their life, they will seek guidance in the wise selection of a name. With increasing frequency numerologists are being consulted to advise on suitable names for professionals, as well as for newborn babes, businessmen or even for people who find that life is not as kind to them as they feel it should be. Indeed, an important vacancy exists in the offices of most theatrical agents, corporate organisations, marriage counsellors and the like for a qualified numerologist whose role would include personality analysis along with name suitability advice.

When considering the acceptability of a name for a person or for an organisation we take into account the following factors: a) The name should provide balance to the Birthchart by supplying strengths on the Namechart where weaknesses are revealed on the Birthchart, thereby aiding the person to overcome his natal weaknesses; b) Where strengths appear on the Birthchart, the Namechart should not compound the same power to create an overbalance of too much strength in a particular direction; c) The

Namechart should not have the same arrows as the Birthchart as this will not make for balance.

These points are clearly shown in the following examples:

Keith, Born July 16, 1963

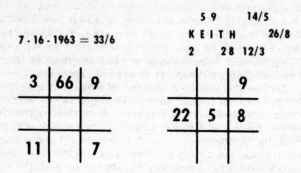

7 - 16 - 1963 = 33/6

$$
\begin{array}{c|c|c}
& 5\ 9 & 14/5 \\
& \text{K E I T H} & 26/8 \\
2 & 28 & 12/3
\end{array}
$$

3	66	9
11		7

		9
22	5	8

The great emphasis indicated by the Birthchart on the mental level is accentuated by the Ruling Number. The major weakness is obviously in the spiritual (feeling) area, indicated by the Arrow of Hypersensitivity. Choosing the name Keith is a great help to this child's sensitivity, giving balance by the addition of the Arrow of Emotional Balance on the Namechart. Further help comes from the Complete Name Number (8), and the Soul Urge Number (5), both of which are feeling numbers. At the same time there is minimal mental emphasis contributed by the name, thereby avoiding over-balance in this direction. In conclusion, it would be hard to think of a more suitable name than Keith for the child born with the birthdate of July 16, 1963.

Charles, Born December 7, 1974

12 - 7 - 1974 = 31/4

$$
\begin{array}{c c c}
1 & 5 & 6 \\
\text{C H A R L E S} & & 30/3 \\
3\ 8 & 9\ 3 & 1 & 24/6
\end{array}
$$

		9
2		
11	4	77

33		9
	5	8
11		

With a Ruling Number of 4 and with such a heavy weight of power on the Practical Plane of the Birthchart, it is wise to avoid a Name Number of 1, 4, 7 or 10, or overweighing the Practical Plane of the Namechart with too many numbers. Charles is fitting here as it adds only two 1s in the practical area. More significantly, such a name provides great mental strength to compensate for its absence in the Birthchart, Ruling Number and Day Number. Charles has its Complete Name Number, Soul Urge and Outer Expression Numbers all on the Mental Plane. Its Namechart provides all the numbers which are missing on the Birthchart, except 6. However, 6 appears in the name as both the Soul Urge and Outer Expression. An extremely unsuitable name for this child would be David. As an exercise, analyse it and see just how strong it is on the Practical Plane. Notice also how it over-balances the individual's power in an extremely materialistic direction, with so little on the Spiritual and Mental Planes to compensate.

ADVICE TO PARENTS

There are many advantages in patiently waiting until babies have arrived before choosing their first names. Although it is wise to have a selection of desirable names in readiness, it is unwise to make the final choice until the day of birth. Not until then will the natal characteristics of the children become numerologically analysable.

Encouraging the patient parents to prepare a short list of acceptable names has many advantages. The resultant names will, in a very subtle way, project harmony to the parents. This is highly important for the parents must feel at ease with the names they are to call their children or they will not use them — then they will have no influence. Choosing a short list of names also gives the parents the opportunity to express their personal preference and, naturally, all parents want to do that. A third advantage of the short list is the time it saves the numerologist. Analysing hundreds of names to select one or two suitable ones is a tedious and time consuming task.

Sometimes compromises have to be reached between numerologically ideal names and those which are pleasing to the ears of mother and father. For instance, if the parents of the child born on December 7, 1974 (as used in the previous example) express a pronounced dislike of the name Charles, then it is not to be considered. If they do not like a suggested name, no matter how ideal its numerological value, when it is unused the value is negated.

The chosen names cannot be abbreviated without impairing the numerologist's work. If the parents of the previous example agree to the name Charles and then shorten it to Chuck or Chas, an important part of its value is missing. The parents must be fully prepared to use the complete name if it is chosen. Otherwise, it would be more desirable to analyse and choose, if suitable, the abbreviated name. Perhaps the full name could then be used for formal purposes.

Many are the occasions when people are given a formal name which is seldom used. Bill, for example, bears no relationship numerologically or phonetically to William; nor does Dick to Richard. These factors must be considered in depth and the intended abbreviation or nick-name always analysed. If suitable, its formal counterpart can still be used for the christening and the birth certificate — but remember, it has no influence unless it is used in everyday communication.

CHANGING A NAME

We all know people who have disliked their first name. At school, children have preferred to accept some nick-name or abbreviated name bestowed upon them by classmates. Later in life a person may decide to formally change his or her first name for personal or professional reasons. Another name might sound more distinctive in general or promotional usage. Whatever the reason, a change in name will gradually produce some corresponding change in the personality.

Many hitherto unknown yet talented people have been known to change their name(s) as a prelude to achieving notable success in the arts — particularly in music and acting. Such examples have been commonplace in Hollywood for as long as Hollywood has been the movie capital of the world. Among the examples is Clark Gable whose first name was actually William.

In the world of music name changes are not unusual. Leopold Stokowski's surname was Stanislaw, before he became one of the most famous orchestral conductors of this century. Dame Nellie Melba, born Helen Mitchell, became the most famous soprano in the world during the early part of this century.

Name changes in the literary world are no less numerous. Author Lewis Carroll was born Charles Lutwidge Dodgson; Mark Twain was born Samuel Clemens; French dramatist Jean Moliere was born Jean Poquelin; Russian novelist Maxim Gorki was born Aleksey Maximovich Pyeshkov. It seems to be an international habit of long standing.

The observant student will note here that probably not one of the foregoing people sought the guidance of a numerologist in making their name changes. In most cases it is safe to say they were changes guided by their own intuition. And we know that genuine intuition is probably the most reliable form of guidance. But today, with so many experts offering opinions and so many materialistic agencies flooding our consciousnesses with rubbish, our psychic powers are often unable to flow unobstructedly and we are very much in need of accurate, reliable and scientific guidance. This is where the science of numbers proves its value.

More than ever before, people are seeking the advice of numerologists about their names. Artists, composers, writers and even students trying to improve their comprehension have all been clients of mine over the past two decades. One very memorable occasion was when a budding young painter sought guidance in the changing of his name. He was experiencing failure after frustrating failure in having his paintings accepted for important exhibitions. He liked the new name and the method of selecting it so well that he enrolled immediately in my forthcoming twelve-week course in numerology. By the time the course was scheduled to commence, two months later, he had so many commissions to paint for exhibitions that he had no time to attend the lectures.

It is not that the change of name will necessarily alter an artist's style. Instead its benefit lies in allowing such a slight modification to the personality that one feels as though a trigger has been released and some small inhibition has been swept aside, permitting the expression to flow freely. Such a minor factor in the personality is often the only barrier between success and mediocrity.

Reasons for changing names are not limited to fame or fortune. How many kings, queens, princes, dukes, earls, lords and others associated with royalty and the peerage undertake name changes? The most famous of all modern name changes in this category is that undertaken by the British Royal House in 1917. From its Germanic origins of Saxe-Coburg-Gotha came the House of Windsor. Many reasons are given in history for such a dramatic change in name, but numerologically we can see that it was not such a wise move. Windsor is strong in determination and in willpower, but is a weak name in terms of planning, action and expression of ideals, by comparison to the previous longer name. So we wonder: was it coincidental that this same period in history saw the commencement of the decline in British superiority and worldwide political and cultural dominance?

Back further in time, we find a change of name to be instrumental in the development of Christianity. Observe in Genesis 17 of the Bible perhaps the two most important name changes in history: Abraham at 100 years of age was told to change his name from Abram; his wife, Sarah, at ninety, was told to change her name from Sarai and that in so doing their union would be fruitful after all those years of barrenness, and she would bring forth a child (Isaac).

Perhaps this practice might be considered by childless couples

165

today. To change a name is to change something of the personality. Since a wise change is based on the removal of emotional blockages, its chances of success could be surprisingly high.

NAME CHANGES IN MARRIAGE

In these days of striving for equality of the sexes, we might ask why it is that the wives are the ones who must change names in marriage. The answer seems to be tradition. So far as the scientific aspect of name changing is concerned, it is of minor importance as to who actually changes the name in marriage, so long as one partner does.

As well as requiring that it be founded on love, marriage must also depend for its success on understanding, trust and harmony between the partners. The challenge is to find harmony in the swiftest, most permanent manner. This is one of the most difficult adjustments people have to make in life, yet it is one which succeeds to an impressively high degree. When two newly-married people settle down to sharing the same home, the same meals, the same life-style, they find it involves far more than sharing the same bed or merely living together as single partners for a time. The difference lies in the permanence afforded by the marriage ceremony and, most importantly, in sharing the same surname.

Unmarried couples who have lived together for some time before deciding to marry are always at a loss to explain the differences in their attitudes which emerge after the ceremony. Adjusting to this new state, even though they lived together beforehand, can be quite demanding. But as their personalities draw more closely together adjustment becomes easier, facilitated to a great extent by the sharing of the same family name.

Hollywood-style marriages seem unique in possessing a record for the highest failure rate. Partners of such marital unions are so often acting as other personalities that they lose contact with their own Inner Self, without which they cannot discover the real meaning of love. By maintaining their pre-marriage names, these people resist the unifying influence of sharing a common surname, one of the primary requirements for a successful marriage. It is impossible to become part of a successful marital union and still maintain total independence.

By now it must be apparent that people's names are not merely sounds by which their attention is attracted. In using them, sets of vibrations are energised which exert varying degrees of influence upon their owners. We are equipped now to gauge the nature and extent of such influences and it behooves us to use the power of names with wisdom and with care.

166

STAGE 13
Compatibility of Ruling Numbers

As a consultant nutritionist I find the cause of the majority of my patients' health problems emanating from some emotional disharmony. A classic example is the case of the elderly couple who came to me with severe indigestion problems early in 1978. Although well into their sixties, this couple was following quite a well-balanced diet of natural foods. Nevertheless they both suffered from acute indigestion after almost every meal. They appeared to be well adjusted to each other, with no perceptible conflict in their general conversation or in their discussion with me about their diet. However my intuition told me I was only hearing a small fraction of the full story.

On setting up their Birthcharts and Ruling Numbers I became speedily aware of the real problem. Deep conflict existed between the personalities of these two people. As they had lived together in a marital situation for some forty years, it was not surprising that they had learned to adjust to each other on a superficial level. But deep down I found a very different picture emerging. The husband was intensely emotional, highly sensitive and artistic. The wife, on the other hand, was exceptionally forceful, with a powerful determination and an analytical brain which related everything to reason. She had no use for feelings — to her, everything that was not rooted in reason was useless.

That they had continued to live in apparent harmony was largely due to his capitulation in most matters, 'for the sake of the children' he said. But they had all left home and were now married, and he was lonelier than ever, still deprived of loving warmth and attention. His wife wanted mental stimulation which he could not provide so she cultivated a wide circle of outside friends to facilitate this. She did not seem to be aware of his needs, nor he of hers.

This couple had now reached the stage in their lives where they should be able to enjoy retirement and the freedom to travel wherever and whenever they wished. Instead they had not even learned how to enjoy each other's company. He was a highly intuitive ruling 5 Piscean with difficulty in verbal self-expression, yet

167

hopefully seeking the opportunity to express himself. She was a ruling 8 Arian, with a heavy accumulation of numbers on the Mind Plane of her Birthchart and the Arrow of Determination. She also possessed a fluent command of self-expression.

It was not difficult for these two intelligent people to follow my explanations of wherein their disharmony lay and how they could overcome it. Neither would believe that their indigestion arose from the clash of their personalities. Still, they were both prepared to try a few important changes in attitude which I knew would help. I asked them to call me the following week to tell me the results of their changes in attitude toward each other. I recommended no change in their physical diet, only in their mental one.

Two very surprised people took turns in speaking to me by phone the following week. They admitted that such simple things as learning to understand each other's true needs and spending a few minutes each day in meditation together could bring about quite a remarkable alteration in their feelings toward each other. They could now eat without the discomfort of acute indigestion after their meals. In fact, they even enjoyed dining out twice together that past week — a thing they had not done for some years.

At the consultation I had explained to them that they were of very different Ruling Numbers, with a wide variation in attitudes to life and its expression. They could see this very clearly when I explained it with the aid of the Birthcharts. I also pointed out something of their karmic need in being together — to learn co-operation and harmonious co-habitation. If they failed this time around they would have to do it again and again until they learned to see the beauty of each other's being and to broaden their attitudes to life. Such important lessons as they had to teach each other could only be digested if each was prepared to give a little.

Very often we find married couples brought together for reasons which seem to be far deeper than merely the pleasure of physical and mental intercourse. We never cease to be amazed upon numerologically analysing the birthdates of many married couples at the disharmony in their basic characteristics and personalities. Obviously marriage has much more to teach us in the delicate art of personality adjustment than we realise.

With so much to learn in life, we have usually attained maturity before gaining sufficient understanding to wisely select a compatible marriage partner. For many people, this does not take place until the second or third marriage. Young people about to marry are often too headstrong and brash to be guided by older and wiser counsel and too immature to consider the importance of employing such accurate means of self-analysis as that provided by numerology and astrology. Yet these proven metaphysical sciences are available for everyone to use in their journey through life.

A marriage partner should be like one's other self. It is the most important association we establish on earth. Consequently we should be far more rational about it than to believe emotional love to be all. Love is that state of being within us which extends to everyone we know; but that special love we feel for our consort, or intended consort, should be always supportable by a numerological analysis of their birthdate.

Of all the numerological factors which influence the depth of human relationships the most powerful are the Ruling Numbers. The next most influential factors are the pattern of numbers on the Birthchart, the Day Numbers, the Personal Year Numbers and finally, the Name Numbers. This order is intended as a basic guide, but if conspicuous strengths or weaknesses show up, they would naturally become of prime importance. Be that as it may, the Ruling Numbers provide the most significant guide to compatibility between two people contemplating marriage.

When we consider that there are eleven different Ruling Numbers, nine spaces on the Birthchart with up to six or seven variations of number compounding in each space, twelve different Day Numbers, nine different Personal Year Numbers, eleven different Soul Urge Numbers, twelve different Outer Expression Numbers and eleven different Complete Name Numbers, we face literally thousands of number combinations representing just as many diverse combinations of human personalities.

Space does not permit us to consider all the possibilities here. But we certainly can investigate the combinations of the most influential of them, the Ruling Numbers. With eleven possible Ruling Numbers, the number of possible combinations between two people is 121 (eleven times eleven).

There are not, however, 121 different compatibility ratings between two people, for there are far too many factors to take into account, as indicated above. Instead, we shall simplify the compatibility ratings of the Ruling Numbers into four basic grades, employing as our guidelines for assessment those characteristics of Ruling Numbers detailed in Stage 4.

Compatibility Ratings of Ruling Numbers

Wherever the letter A appears in a square on the chart overleaf, it indicates that the two Ruling Numbers forming that square have the highest potential compatibility rating. The letter B indicates a compatibility rating not as high as A, but higher than C. The lowest compatibility rating between two Ruling Numbers is indicated by the letter D — this does not imply total disharmony, but rather that the two people involved must recognise their wide differences and co-operate all the more to overcome them.

If you and your partner have Ruling Numbers which combine to give you an A rating, you know that your compatibility potential is a maximum one. Unless there are other strong factors to detract from your harmonising together, you should be a delightfully happy pair. A B rating would indicate that you have a seventy-five percent compatibility potential compared to the A, with a few more personality conflicts to overcome than with an A rating.

The compatibility rating of the C combinations is about fifty percent that of the A potential, indicating that these people must employ much more diligence in adjusting to each other for a happy marriage.

The lowest compatibility potential, that indicated by the D ratings as about twenty-five percent, provides the climate in which the marriage participants must work the hardest for a happy association. Surprising as it might seem, some of the best adjusted married couples are found within this grouping, for it is they who have tried most diligently to work together and have thoroughly learned how to give and take to achieve a successful union. This is a further testimony of the old axiom that the harder you have to work for something, the more you appreciate it.

RULING NUMBERS	2	3	4	5	6	7	8	9	10	11	22/4
2	B	B	A	C	A	B	D	B	C	B	A
3	B	A	C	C	A	C	C	A	D	C	B
4	A	C	B	D	B	A	A	C	A	C	B
5	C	C	D	B	C	C	D	B	A	B	C
6	A	A	B	C	A	C	C	A	C	B	D
7	B	C	A	C	C	B	D	B	A	B	A
8	D	C	A	D	C	D	C	C	B	B	A
9	B	A	C	B	A	B	C	A	D	B	B
10	C	D	A	A	C	A	B	D	B	D	C
11	B	C	C	B	B	B	B	B	D	B	A
22/4	A	B	B	C	D	A	A	B	C	A	B

STAGE 14
Numerology, E.S.P. and Intuition

The science of numbers is an intensely practical system designed to provide a unique insight into human personality and its potential, but it is much more than that. It is a valuable means whereby our intuition and extrasensory perception (E.S.P.) can develop to the point of becoming controlled, workable instruments in attaining improved all-round psychic awareness. Such awareness extends beyond physical limitations.

Everyone possesses the paraphysical senses of E.S.P. and intuition. However, not everyone is aware of these. Preoccupation with the physical tends to hamper the awakening of such consciousness. Gradually, through repeated flashes of insight, we become aware that it is possible to attain knowledge of an event before its actual occurrence. This is part of intuition. On other occasions, we become conscious of other people's thoughts or of conflicts in their emotional makeup. These we detect through our extrasensory perception.

Intuition is a very comprehensive sense. In popular usage it is a word employed to cover any sense or feeling beyond the ordinary which might be interpreted as a personal guide. This is rather inaccurate because it tends to confuse intuition and E.S.P. Although these two senses are closely related, they have very definite fields of application. Intuition comes before thought. It manifests itself in momentary flashes only because thought takes over. Thought then either accepts and develops the intuitive impulse or else rationalises and rejects it. The selection is determined by our earthly conditioning.

On the other hand, E.S.P. depends on the user being in a state of relaxation. This allows the mind to be extended and projected to other sources of vibration, particularly human, although it also encompasses spiritual, animal, mineral and plant energy fields. (A source of vibration creates around it an energy field which reveals the essence and quality condition of that source.) Having met with a particular energy field the mind transmits the impressions back to the brain; the brain translates these into comprehensible terms.

171

In practice we find the general term of intuition covers such faculties as first impressions, foreknowledge, premonitions and pre-conceptions. These invariably must be accepted on faith, for they can rarely be rationalised. Extending into a further dimension, E.S.P. depends on the mind's engagement of the brain to interpret the impressions. The domains of extrasensory perception encompass clairvoyance, clairaudience, psychometry and mental telepathy.

The most important aspect of E.S.P. insofar as numerology is concerned, is its value in detecting powerful prevailing vibrations. Extrasensory perception is both a guide and a protector. By its ability to perceive strong sources of energy it acts as a tocsin, warning of harmful emotional turbulence created by such reactions as anger, hatred and lust. This indicates to the experienced numerologist critical problem areas for correction. Through its telepathic faculties E.S.P. also provides a means of mental contact with the subject being analysed, a contact which is crystallised when the person's numerological pattern is established through his Birthchart.

In man's pristine state his metaphysical senses were his means of being alerted to anything which might endanger his safety and also of receiving constructive guidance. With his later development of mental faculties he tended to disparage these higher senses as he became more and more enchanted with the physical world. By relying exclusively upon his physical senses and his reasoning faculties, man's senses of higher perception atrophied from neglect. Recognising this, new age man is taking measures to achieve a balance between his sensory and rational faculties. Strong forces are leading him to restore the equilibrium because of his innate yearning for the Edenic state.

Intuition and E.S.P. are regarded as metaphysical senses as they both function at higher frequency levels and are of a much finer nature than the five physical senses. They require more alertness and finer attunement for their reliable operation. Intuition is really our sixth sense because, to a greater or lesser degree, it is common to everyone. E.S.P. should be regarded as the seventh sense, for it comes with greater sensitivity and awareness. As we engage in regular practice with the science of numbers, our precognitive senses of intuition and E.S.P. are being subtly but regularly employed. With every analysis, we grow a little more aware of the vast creative plan of life as it is expressed through each individual. Gradually numerology becomes a means of comprehending the limitlessness of creation exemplified through human expression and awareness.

To the intelligent person nothing is more exhilarating than to engage in something which expands the consciousness. Applied numerology is so satisfying in this regard that there is an early tendency towards overenthusiasm. That early excitement, arising from discovering insights into the secrets of the Inner Self, must be contained to avoid the errors of judgement which inevitably accompany immaturity in any field. Especially with a psychic science, we must exercise great restraint to avoid the temptation of jumping to hasty conclusions. Any early errors will, of course, rapidly teach the thinking person to be more discreet and to embrace greater diplomacy in revealing the results of his analyses. Such slips should not be regarded as mistakes or failures (either of the person or the system) but rather as lessons intended to develop our understanding.

The blossoming of our greater awareness brings with it a progressively more uncanny accuracy in our assessment of the person being analysed. Our metaphysical senses are now coming into greater spontaneous use, with a noticeable sharpening of the intuition and of our ability to link up with the subject (extrasensory contact). How this works is perhaps no better illustrated than by one of the many examples of intuition and E.S.P. in action demonstrated at most of our regular students' class nights.

One evening, Toni seemed to waft into the classroom on a wave of sheer exhilaration. When asked why she appeared so elated, she told us she was in love!

What more practical exercise could we attempt that evening than to analyse the birthdates of Toni and her new beau? She was more than willing, volunteering to set up the Birthcharts and Pyramids on the blackboard herself. As Toni finished and stood back, some of the class members made comments on the harmony between the two Birthcharts, the Ruling Numbers and the Sun Signs of Toni and her love. Without any comment from Toni, or previous knowledge of her friend, I asked how she thought she would cope with his children. The class was thunderstruck. Toni wanted to know how I knew he had been married and had children. I said that I had had no prior information, and actually did not know whether he was still married or divorced, or how many children he had, but I was sure that he felt a heavy responsibility toward them and Toni could, at best, only occupy second place to them in his heart. I also 'saw' that he had a health problem. It was clear from his numbers that he was insecure and had, I felt, a problem with alcoholism. But Toni assured us she was helping him with that.

'He is too dogmatic and orthodox,' I advised her. 'Your role as a reformer will only be temporary, but do try.'

She tried — and failed. They have since separated. Both learned much from the love match while it lasted. But by being forewarned (not conditioned), Toni did not feel too upset when the break came.

The class learned much, too, especially about intuition. There was no other way by which I could have known about his children except by attuning to the man himself through his formula: his numbers as set out on the Birthcharts and Pyramids. This is priceless intuition in action.

Every successful numerologist has achieved proficiency through the ability to see beyond the form of numbers — to see into their essence, as it were. Relying solely on the information conveyed by the actual numbers of the charts will, of itself, provide valuable guidance. But to delve beyond this information uncovers important insights not otherwise obtainable. This faculty proved to be of precious value to a friend of mine, a most capable numerologist who was nearly arrested by police on false charges.

Mrs Wellington had a weekly radio talkback programme on which she would advise parents on the handling of problems with their children. Parents would receive such accurate and spontaneous assessments of the child's temperament, health and idiosyncrasies that the astonished mother would often question how Mrs Wellington could possibly know the child so well. Mrs Wellington would give a brief explanation of the science of numbers as being her source of information about the child being analysed. Apparently all did not believe her because some people accused her of witchcraft — not that they took issue with her advice, but rather with the unfathomable manner in which she obtained it. Some accused her of dabbling in the occult as well as with witchcraft. In that state, such accusations implied a crime against society.

As she walked out of her broadcasting studio one afternoon, Mrs Wellington was approached by two burly gentlemen. One introduced himself as the inspector of police, the other was his sergeant. They were required to report, they said, on the methods Mrs Wellington used to obtain the information she broadcast over the radio about children she had never seen. The poor lady was deeply shocked. For a few minutes she was unable to speak. That anyone could be so distrustful of her methods or her intent quite floored Mrs Wellington. While leading the policemen into her office, Mrs Wellington wondered how she could prove to them in a few moments the methods she had spent half a lifetime in developing. Suddenly, as though in answer to her prayer, she asked the inspector his date of birth. 'You see, she said to the inspector, 'I use a system called the science of numbers. This gives me a very accurate guide to any person by merely knowing their birthdate.'

The inspector was clearly not impressed; nevertheless, he gave her his birthdate. Mrs Wellington set the birthdate on a chart and almost immediately turned to the inspector. She told him that he did not really want to join the police force, that as a youth he yearned to become a surgeon but his father could not afford to send him to university. She told him that his father was a railway worker but had died some years previously. As the father had never earned more than a modest wage, he could do no better for his son, his only son, than to send him to join the police force. The inspector was wide-eyed. He could barely believe what he heard. How could this lady, whom he had never met before, know so much about his early life? He asked her a few questions about himself, to which she replied in great detail, giving him an accurate analysis of his personality. By the time she had finished, Mrs Wellington knew that she had convinced the policemen of the reliability of her methods, for they were both looking at her dumbfounded. She told the inspector that she hoped he would act as righteously and as sensitively as was natural to him, which she saw revealed in his Birthchart.

Instead of a brief official visit which would possibly have led to an arrest, the inspector and his assistant remained with Mrs Wellington for an hour and a half. During this time she gave both men a complete analysis of their wives and their children, even to the extent of helping the sergeant with a particular problem he had with a backward child (he had said nothing of this, but she detected the problem early in their meeting through her acutely sensitive E.S.P.). Perhaps the most important measure of Mrs Wellington's success was the offer by these two policemen to pay her for her analyses. She, of course, refused, but was assured that she would never again be troubled by the police in her work.

It is true that not everyone can develop intuitiveness and E.S.P. to the same penetrating degree. The vital factors determining the successful unfolding of these senses are related to a person's own level of spiritual attunement. This is fundamentally determined by the amount of spiritual strength available to them as indicated by the Spiritual Plane of their Birthchart, by their Ruling Number and to a lesser extent, by the spiritual factors in their name. People with two 2s on their Birthchart have a higher chance of achieving success in developing their psychic senses with less effort than those not so favourably endowed. However, it is very often more a matter of what you do with your talents than what you have been given. For example, Mrs Wellington was a person with only one 2 on her Birthchart. Her early life was one of intense and unremitting struggle to maintain a large family as a widow. She succeeded because she was highly intelligent (although with a poor academic education) and spiritually very alert — in fact, she had developed a very accurate intuition.

Of this every reader may be sure: if you did not have the potential for advanced psychic awareness, you would have lost interest in the subject of numerology long before now. You would certainly not have read this far into the book.

We must always realise that our emerging psychic awareness can only blossom when our values are altruistic. If personal gain, unfair advantage, or other unworthy motives underlie our purpose in learning or in applying this science, our success would be hampered by a unique aspect of spiritual law which seems to stand guardian over life's esoteric knowledge: the more we learn, the greater our responsibility for that knowledge. Our life, therefore, must itself be an example of truth and wisdom in action. For if our metaphysical senses are to develop to a point of reliable guidance, our emotions must always be under control, our mental processes must always be clear and unpolluted. Pure guidance has never been known to come through confused, cluttered or corrupt pathways.

We find many people go through life blatantly unaware of the conflict they create within themselves when they fail to live in accord with their words and thoughts. To act hypocritically is to commit a most grievous mischief to yourself. Perhaps you might avoid the laws of the land or even remain undetected by your fellows, but of this you may be sure: your higher self knows everything that is going on and maintains this knowledge on record. Ultimately, every misdemeanor must be expiated — such is the irrevocable nature of the law of compensation. Remember, the greatest sin of all is to be untrue to oneself. The science of numbers will equip you with an accurate and practical means of self-analysis. In applying this knowledge, you can end any semblance of haphazard living. Life no longer has to be the difficult steering of your ship through uncharted waters.

You will never be the same again. Does anyone regret that?